The Body of Christ as Seen through the Eyes of a Physician

The Body of Christ as Seen through the Eyes of a Physician

PAT FOSARELLI, MD, DMIN

CASCADE *Books* · Eugene, Oregon

THE BODY OF CHRIST AS SEEN THROUGH THE EYES
OF A PHYSICIAN

Cascade Books
An Imprint of Wipf and Stock Publishers
199 W. 8th Ave., Suite 3
Eugene, OR 97401

www.wipfandstock.com

PAPERBACK ISBN: 978-1-6667-6542-7
HARDCOVER ISBN: 978-1-6667-6543-4
EBOOK ISBN: 978-1-6667-6544-1

Cataloguing-in-Publication data:

Names: Fosarelli, Pat. | author

Title: The Body of Christ as Seen through the Eyes of a Physician / Pat Fosarelli.

Description: Eugene, OR: Cascade Books, 2024 | Includes bibliographical references.

Identifiers: ISBN 978-1-6667-6542-7 (paperback) | ISBN 978-1-6667-6543-4 (hardcover) | ISBN 978-1-6667-6544-1 (ebook)

Subjects: LCSH: Medicine—religious aspects. | Jesus Christ—example. | Spirituality.

Classification: BV 4596.P5 F5 2024 (paperback) | BV 4596.P5 (ebook)

VERSION NUMBER 02/26/25

Contents

Introduction

As a child, I was always confused about the notion that we were all members of the "body of Christ." All I could think of was a huge physical body, and that seemed a bit scary. And how could we be members of that body? We would be swallowed up by the enormity of it! Later on, when I learned that a "body" could also mean a group of people (or a group of anything), I could understand that the body of Christ might simply be a collection of believers, without much interaction with or even relationship to each other.

Yet, that is clearly not what St. Paul had in mind when he wrote to the ancient churches, especially the one at Corinth, about each person being a member of the body of Christ. He stressed that each person has a role and that all members have an effect on each other and the whole body. As a physician, I now recognize that he was speaking about the body of Christ in terms of the human body. A body has many cells making up the whole; they are all united as members of a particular body through the same set of genes. In some way, cells recognize that they share something in common with cells that have the same genes and that they lack that relationship with cells carrying other genes. Furthermore, each group of cells has its own job to do; otherwise, the body will not function properly or will be quite ill, even moribund. Cells must cooperate with similar cells, and groups of cells must cooperate with other groups of cells related to them but not very much like them at all, if optimum health is to be achieved for the whole human body.

Now that I myself am a member of a church named Corpus Christi in Baltimore (*Corpus Christi* is Latin for body of Christ), the thought has occurred to me that, somewhere along the way, most of us have lost sight of the beauty of Paul's words, even in our church communities. It was this belief and the inspiration of my fellow parishioners of Corpus Christi that became the impetus for this work.

In our society, we are tempted to "go it alone," to be an independent individual at all costs. We can be part of a group if it suits us, but we can—and should—jettison participation if our needs are not met *immediately* by such a group, for we are the best judges of what gives us meaning. Why should we be part of someone else's project if it does not primarily serve *us*? The idea of being part of something larger than ourselves—whether it suits our immediate needs or not—seems to be quaint. And so, we tend to hop from one social or political group to another, without even a glance backward. We move from one neighborhood to another, failing to keep in contact with the neighbors we leave (if we ever knew them in the first place).

Perhaps, it is in the area of religious faith that such rootlessness is the most difficult to comprehend. For centuries, people gathered together in faith communities to meet a common goal, much larger than any individual one. It was the norm to stay with one's faith community for life. Now, it is not uncommon for people to move from one church to another—within the same denomination or across denominations—in an attempt to find what "suits" them. A microscopic view has overtaken a panoramic one, as metaphorically speaking, individual trees are seen but the entire forest is missed.

Such a view might work for some organizations, but it clearly doesn't work for the body of Christ, an organic entity, designed by God, in which each person is important and has a vital role to play. Although each person, in the end, is served by the body, the primary focus is what each individual brings to the body, i.e., what gifts, talents, and contributions he or she is uniquely able to provide for the good of all.

Is such a view hopelessly out-of-date in our modern world? I think not, unless we are prepared to argue that the construction of the human body itself is itself an anachronism. After all, most of us do not like it when cells in our own bodies go awry, fail to work, or are transformed into malignancies. We want our cells—different as they might be—to work together so that we (as a whole being) will feel well and actually *be* well.

This book is divided into three parts. In Part I, I begin with the Pauline texts that the church has treasured for over two millennia. In chapter 1, I explore the concept of "body" in the ancient world, the world of Paul, and also provide some background into the Corinthian church, the church that evoked most of Paul's writing about the body of Christ. Chapter 2 is an in-depth exploration of modern biblical scholars' reflections on the body of Christ in Paul's first Letter to the Corinthians and in Paul's letters to the Romans and to the Ephesians. The purpose is to demonstrate the earliest history of the body of Christ as community.

Part II (chapter 3) highlights the church's tradition of the body of Christ as community. Although many (if not most) church fathers had much to say on this theme, in the interest of space, only several church leaders can be covered in this chapter, with examples of other leaders' teachings found in the Appendix. The purpose is to illustrate the developing history of the body of Christ as community and, in the process, to encourage readers to embrace the very organic spirituality of interdependence with each other and dependence on God.

In Part III, I provide some metaphorical comparisons between the human body and what ails it, and the body of Christ and what ails it. This section begins with a description of a "Corpus Christi" spirituality (chapter 4) and the way that the body of Christ is built up today (chapter 5). Part III continues with an exploration of the body of Christ and the various ailments that can affect it, using comparisons taken directly from the human body. I explore extrinsic threats to the body of Christ, such as woundedness (chapter 6) and pathogens and toxins (chapter 7), while in the following sections of Part III, I explore internal threats to the body, such as malignancy (chapter 8), failure of heart (chapter 9), and malnutrition (chapter 10). Chapter 11 concludes this work by presenting a vision for the interaction of the body of Christ with the world. I offer my view on how adherence to the concept of the body of Christ might, for Christians, be a remedy against the rampant individualism, secularism, and consumerism of our time, mind-sets that can tear our solidarity asunder, not just in terms of socioeconomic or ethnic realities (e.g., rich vs. poor; white vs. black; young vs. old; men vs. women), but even among people who share the same characteristics. If there is no common goal, everything is up to each individual's judgment. In such a view, even our best friend's goals might threaten our own. Certainly, God's goals might be at odds with ours. Lacking an encompassing view or goal, we run the risk of trivializing life itself.

Each chapter will have questions for individual and group reflection to promote a spirituality of interconnectedness with each other and with Christ. My hope is that all who learn more about the magnificent interrelatedness inherent in the body of Christ will be spiritually challenged to live this reality in their personal, social, and professional lives, so that we really may manifest ourselves as "Corpus Christi" in our world today.

Finally, I am indebted to Emile Mersch's 1938 work, *The Whole Christ*, an excellent resource that I will quote liberally throughout certain chapters.

The Pauline Texts that Refer to the Body of Christ

(All biblical texts are the New American Bible (NAB) translations)

CORINTHIANS

1 Corinthians 10:16–17—(16) The cup of blessing that we bless, is it not a participation in the blood of Christ? The bread that we break, is it not a participation in the body of Christ? (17) Because the loaf of bread is one, **we, though many, are one body,** for we all partake of the same loaf.

1 Corinthians 12:4–7; 12–27—(4) There are different kinds of spiritual gifts but the same Spirit; (5) there are different forms of service but the same Lord; (6) there are different workings but the same God who produces all of them in everyone. (7) To each individual, the manifestation of the Spirit is given for some benefit . . . (12) **As a body is one though it has many parts, and all the parts of the body, though many, are one body, so also Christ. (13) For in one Spirit, we were all baptized into one body,** whether Jews or Greeks, slaves or free persons, and we were all given to drink of the one Spirit. **(14) Now the body is not a single part, but many. (15) If a foot should say, "Because I am not a hand, I do not belong to the body," it does not for this reason belong any less to the body. (16) Or if an ear should say, "because I am not an eye, I do not belong to the body," it does not for this reason belong any less to the body. (17) If the whole body were an eye, where would the hearing be? If the whole body were hearing, where would the** sense of smell be? (18) But as it is, God placed the parts, each one of them, in the body as he intended. (19) If they were all one part, where would the body be? (20) But as it is, there are many parts, yet one body. (21) The eye cannot say to the hand, "I do not need you," nor the head to the feet, "I do not need you." (22) Indeed, the parts of the body that seem the weaker are all the more necessary, (23) and those parts of the body that we consider less honorable, we surround with greater honor, and our less presentable parts are treated with greater propriety, (24) whereas our more presentable parts do not need this. But God has so constructed the body as to give greater honor to a part that is without it, (25) so that there may be no division in the body, but that the parts may have the same concern for one another. (26) If [one] part suffers, all the parts suffer with it; if one part is honored, all the parts share its joy. (27) Now you are Christ's body, and individually parts of it.

ROMANS

Romans 7:4—In the same way, you were also put to death to the law through **the body of Christ, so that you might belong to another,** to the one who was raised from the dead in order that we might bear fruit for God.

Romans 12:4–6—(4) **For as in one body, we have many parts, and all the parts do not have the same function, (5) so we, though many, are one body in Christ and individually parts of one another.** (6) Since we have gifts that differ according to the grace given us, let us exercise them.

EPHESIANS

Ephesians 1:22—And he put all things beneath his feet and gave him as head over all thing to **the church, which is his body**, the fullness of the one who fills all things in every way.

Ephesians 4:1–7; 11–13; 15–16—(1) I, then, a prisoner for the Lord, urge you to live in a manner worthy of the call you have received, (2) with all humility and gentleness, with patience, bearing with one another through love, (3) striving to preserve the unity of the spirit through the bond of peace: (4) **one body and one Spirit**, . . . (5) one Lord, one faith, one baptism; (6) one God and Father of all, who is over all and through all and in all. (7) But grace was given to each of us according to the measure of Christ's gift . . . (11) And he gave some as apostles, others as prophets, others as evangelists, others as pastors and teachers, (12) to equip the holy ones for the work of ministry, for **building up the body of Christ**, (13) until we all attain the unity of faith and knowledge of the Son of God, to mature manhood, to the extent of the full stature of Christ . . . (15) Rather, living the truth in love, we should grow in every way into him who is **the head, Christ, (16) from whom the whole body, joined and held together by every supporting ligament, with the proper functioning of each part, brings about the body's growth** and builds itself up in love.

Ephesians 5:29–30—(29) No one heats his own flesh but rather nourishes it and cherishes it, even as Christ does **the church, (30) because we are members of his body**.

COLOSSIANS

Colossians 1:24—I rejoice in my sufferings for your sake, and in my flesh, I am filling up what is lacking in the afflictions of Christ on behalf of **his body, which is the church** . . .

Chapter 1

Background

PAUL OF TARSUS WAS a man of contrasts. Devout Jew, devout follower of Christ; persecutor of Christians, Christian martyr; forceful preacher, humble servant. The authentic letters of Paul present a man who was very complicated, yet single-hearted in his devotion to Christ.

The phrase "body of Christ" as a reference to the community of those who followed Christ did not appear in any of the Gospels or Acts of the Apostles. It was Paul who coined the usage in his letters, which were written long before the Gospels. To better understand what Paul meant two thousand years ago, and in order to put his words into action today, some background is in order with regard to 1) the meaning of "body" in Paul's time and 2) the church at Corinth, to whose members much of Paul's teaching on the body of Christ was written.

THE BODY IN ANTIQUITY

The ancients believed that the human body was arranged hierarchically, with the soul or mind having the greatest status, which included governance over the rest of the body. As Martin noted, "Body hierarchy often expressed itself in the ways in which Greco-Roman writers explained the dynamics of the body's innards. The body's parts, humors, fluids, and forces were pictured as agents or aspects of a social economy, and their interaction was described in terms of political power struggles."[1]

In addition to its meaning as the physical form of an individual human being, "body" could mean the body politic. The earliest such usage of which we are aware came from India in *The Mahabharata* (XIV, xxii), in which the mind and organs of perception debate, the metaphoric point being that ignorance of how members of society must cooperate leads to human arrogance.[2]

The Greeks

The Greeks popularized the "body" theme, and all the great Greek philosophers used it in their writings. For example, in *Laws* (628c ff), Plato characterized "the highest good as a peaceful, friendly state, like a healthy body that does not require medical attention."[3] In *Politics* (1253a), Aristotle noted that "'the state is by nature clearly prior to the family and the individual' . . . . society, therefore, is a creation of nature not of man." Hence, if the state is destroyed, so will families and individuals: "if the whole body be destroyed, there will be no foot or hand."[4] In Xenophon's *Memorabilia* (II, iii), Socrates urged "reconciliation between quarreling brothers by citing the harmony of pairs of hands, feet, and eyes."[5]

One of Aesop's fables concerned the body and how each part must a) do its work or the entire body will languish and b) that a part's importance isn't always obvious.

> Back when all the parts of the human body did not function in unison as is the case today, each member of the body had its own opinion and was able to speak. The various members were offended that everything won by their hard work and diligent efforts was

1. Martin, *Corinthian Body*, 31.
2. Hale, "Analogy of the Body Politic."
3. Hale, "Analogy of the Body Politic."
4. Hale, "Analogy of the Body Politic."
5. Hale, "Analogy of the Body Politic."

delivered to the stomach while he simply sat there in their midst, fully at ease and just enjoying the delights that were brought to him. Finally, the members of the body revolted: the hands refused to bring food to the mouth, the mouth refused to take in any food, and the teeth refused to chew anything. In their angry efforts to subdue the stomach with hunger, the various parts of the body and the whole body itself completely wasted away. As a result, they realized that the work done by the stomach was no small matter, and that the food he consumed was no more than what he gave back to all the parts of the body . . .[6]

In this "political" fable, the body parts that do all the work (i.e., human laborers) become angry at the one part that just sits and eats all day (i.e., the wealthy class). Yet, as the fable points out, in a well-functioning society, as in a well-functioning body, all parts must work together. As noted by Garland in his book on 1 Corinthians, the fable was successfully used by Roman governor Menenius Agrippa in 494 BCE in a speech designed to end a rebellion of plebs in his city by making Aesop's analogy clear. "Drawing a parallel from this to show how like was the internal dissension of bodily members to the anger of the plebs against the fathers, he prevailed upon the minds of his hearers"[7]

The Romans

The Romans continued this usage of "body." In *De offices* (III, 22), the orator Cicero noted that "if each part of the body tries to appropriate the health of the others, then the body will die; such behavior in men would be equally destructive."[8] In *De ira* (II, 31), the philosopher Seneca noted that just as it would be "unnatural for the hands to destroy the feet, so the need for harmony, love,

6. Gibbs, *Aesop's Fables*, 35.

7. Garland, *1 Corinthians*, 594.

8. Hale, "Analogy of the Body Politic."

and mutual protection causes mankind to protect individuals."[9] Thiessen quotes Seneca as saying, "We are parts of one great body. Nature produced us related to one another, since she created us from the same source and to the same end,"[10] while Thiselton noted that in *Moralia* (478D), Plutarch lauded the interdependence of the eyes, ears, hands, and feet of the body, and Epictetus, in *Dissertations* (2.10.4–10.5) praised the "mutual advantage of the harmonious function of the body."[11]

The Jews

Although we cannot be sure what *directly* influenced Paul's usage of "body," it is likely that, at least *indirectly*, Paul was influenced by the prevailing usage of his time, especially by the Hebrew notion of Israel as a corporate personality. Corporate personality refers to thinking about a group of persons as being in solidarity (because of some important attribute, such as family, fellow countrymen), that the group takes on a personality of its own and can even be represented by one specific person, usually a prominent one. For example, in Hosea 6:4, we read, "What should I do with you, Ephraim? What should I do with you, Judah?" These were originally names of people, which Hosea used as signifying a people.

Other examples use the name "Israel." Moses repeatedly used the term "Israel" when he was addressing the people (e.g., Deuteronomy 4:1; 5:1; 6:3, 4; 9:1; 20:3; 27:9; 33:29). In their warnings to the people, the prophets repeatedly used the term "Israel" or "O Israel," underscoring the importance of the corporate body (e.g., Isaiah 40:27; 43:1, 22; 44:21; 49:3; Jeremiah 4:1; 30:10; 46:27; Ezekiel 13:4; 37:1; Hosea 9:1; 10:9; 13:9; 14:1; Amos 4:12; Zephaniah 3:14). References to "Israel" as representing an entire people are also found in the Psalms (50:7; 81:8; 115:9), Exodus (32:4, 8),

9. Hale, "Analogy of the Body Politic."

10. Thiessen, *Psychological Aspects of Pauline Theology*, 328.

11. Thiselton, *The First Epistle to the Corinthians*, 992.

Numbers (24:5), Joshua (7:13), 2 Samuel (20:1), 1 Kings (12:16, 28), and 2 Chronicles (10:16)[12]

Because Paul had been a faithful Jew, this language of corporate personality would have been very familiar to him. As a Jew, he would have appreciated the "both-and" Hebrew idea of being a member of a people, with mutual interdependence of each person with others, while—at the same time—individual responsibility of each person. The individual retained his or her importance even within the corporate personality concept. (As an aside, the doctrine of original sin is based on the idea of the corporate personality of humankind, so that the sin of the first human beings affects all.)

Scholars debate whether the Greek translation of the Old Testament introduced the term "body" into Jewish thought for the first time. The Septuagint uses *soma* (the Greek word for body) multiple times, and most of the time it refers to the whole person. Whenever Paul used *soma* (even without reference to Christ), he used it to refer to the whole person; *soma* is also the word that Paul used when he wrote about the body of Christ. Paul used the word "body" nearly seventy times in the letters to the Corinthians and the Romans.[13]

"While the term 'body' did not originate with him, Paul was apparently the first to apply it to a community, *within* the larger community of the state, and to the *personal* responsibilities of people for one another rather than for more external duties."[14] But Paul's use of this image is different and unique, for unlike the previous examples cited that imply a kind of hierarchy of parts, Paul was "interested in arguing for the necessity of *diversity* within communal unity . . . .for Paul the idea of 'the body of Christ' is *not* a metaphor. He understands the community . . . literally, in some way, to comprise the physical, material, corporeal presence of Christ on earth."[15] In other words, Paul believed that Christ

12. Blue Letter Bible, "O Israel."

13. Bultema, "Soma or Body."

14. Banks, *Paul's Idea of Community*, 70.

15. Hollingshead, *Household of Caesar and the Body of Christ*, 155–56.

actually lives on earth through his diverse community of followers through a real and personal union. Paul was very clear that Christ is the "head" of his body. In terms of the word "head," Paul was likely influenced by the medicine of the day. Although "head" could mean a ruler,

> ". . . the head was the source and center of the life of the body—all that was needed for the proper functioning of the body derived from the head . . . . [Paul] speaks of Christ as the source of our life and, more than that, as the one who sustains and nurtures that life . . . . As against the headship of authority (Old Testament), this physiological metaphor presents what might be described as 'the headship of source and of service' (the head sustaining the life of which it is the source . . . .)"[16]

In other words, Christ has primacy in his body, both giving it life and sustaining its life.

Reflection Questions

1. *When you hear the word "body" used to refer to a group of people, what images or ideas come to mind?*

2. *What do you think of the notion of a "corporate personality"? Would it be possible for modern people to embrace that concept? How might our actions as a nation be different if we really believed that we were a corporate personality?*

CORINTH

Given that Paul's extensive comments on the body of Christ were directed to the Corinthian Christians, some background about the city and its church is in order.

Corinth was an ancient city in Greece, located on an isthmus between the Aegean and Adriatic Seas, about forty-eight miles

16. Williams, *Paul's Metaphors*, 90–91.

southwest of Athens. Because it had two seaports, one facing west and one facing east, it quickly became a cosmopolitan city, as ships and merchants to all parts of the Roman Empire stopped in its harbors. "Corinth was situated as a connecting point between east and west . . . preventing the need [for ships] to sail the treacherous seas around Greece."[17] It was a relatively young city. "Devastated by the Roman army in 146 BC, the Greek city of Corinth was re-founded a century later as a Roman colony (44 BC) . . . . Originally populated by freed slaves, by the mid-first century, the population of Roman Corinth had swelled to nearly 30,000."[18]

Perhaps Paul established the church at Corinth because he was attracted to the socioeconomic mix of persons in such a cosmopolitan location, with their need to hear the good news of Christ.

> While 1 Corinthians addresses the church as a single entity (1 Cor 1:2), the Corinthian church may have contained several cell groups. These ordinarily met in the homes of private individuals (1 Cor 16:19; Rom 16:5; Col 4:15; Phlm 2) and only occasionally came together as a larger group (1 Cor 11:20; 14:23; Rom 16:23). The church was essentially a microcosm of the city. Still in its infancy when Paul wrote, the church contained as few as forty or fifty members . . . . almost certainly there were no more than one or two hundred . . . .[19]

Apparently, the Corinthian congregation had problems with its own diversity of membership, as some of the wealthier members treated poorer members badly, especially at the Lord's Supper (1 Corinthians 11: 17–34). Some members felt that they were special (and that others were not) because of their socioeconomic status, wealth, or gifts of the Spirit. When Paul heard about what was occurring, he sent a letter from where he was staying in Ephesus in about 57 CE to the congregation in Corinth. Although the letter began with Paul thanking God for the grace given to the

17. Brookins, *Reading 1 Corinthians*, 1.

18. Brookins, *Reading 1 Corinthians*, 2.

19. Brookins, *Reading 1 Corinthians*, 3.

Corinthians, he quickly turned to his concerns. Some individuals ("Chloe's people" in 1:11) had reported to Paul that there were rivalries among the Corinthians. Paul's tone in the letter revealed his frustration and anger, especially when he admonished the Corinthians about their bragging about loyalties and spiritual gifts; their sexual misconduct, idolatry, and liturgical abuses, including their behavior at Eucharist, in which the wealthy did not wait for or even include the impoverished, and the unworthy participation at Eucharist by some members. The Corinthians were acting like anything but a unified body! Paul provided his opinions about all of these matters before chapter 12, in which he presented his belief in the body of believers, the body of Christ.

With this background, we turn to the parts of Paul's letter in which he uses body imagery.

Reflection Questions

1. *As it has been described, what does the church at Corinth remind you of?*

2. *Have you ever been in a congregation which behaved like Corinth? Over what issues was the church divided? Did the congregation have strong or weak leadership at the time?*

Chapter 2

What Did Paul Say and Mean in His Letters to the Churches?

THE CHURCH AT CORINTH

1 Corinthians 12:4–7; 12–27—(4) There are different kinds of spiritual gifts but the same Spirit; (5) there are different forms of service but the same Lord; (6) there are different workings but the same God who produces all of them in everyone. (7) To each individual, the manifestation of the Spirit is given for some benefit . . . **(12) As a body is one though it has many parts, and all the parts of the body, though many, are one body, so also Christ. (13) For in one Spirit, we were all baptized into one body,** whether Jews or Greeks, slaves or free persons, and we were all given to drink of the one Spirit. **(14) Now the body is not a single part, but many. (15) If a foot should say, "Because I am not a hand, I do not belong to the body," it does not for this reason belong any less to the body. (16) Or if an ear should say, "because I am not an eye, I do not belong to the body," it does not for this reason belong any less to the body. (17) If the whole body were an eye, where would the hearing be?**

If the whole body were hearing, where would the sense of smell be? (18) But as it is, God placed the parts, each one of them, in the body as he intended. (19) If they were all one part, where would the body be? (20) But as it is, there are many parts, yet one body. (21) The eye cannot say to the hand, "I do not need you," nor the head to the feet, "I do not need you." (22) Indeed, the parts of the body that seem the weaker are all the more necessary, (23) and those parts of the body that we consider less honorable, we surround with greater honor, and our less presentable parts are treated with greater propriety, (24) whereas our more presentable parts do not need this. But God has so constructed the body as to give greater honor to a part that is without it, (25) so that there may be no division in the body, but that the parts may have the same concern for one another. (26) If [one] part suffers, all the parts suffer with it; if one part is honored, all the parts share its joy. (27) Now you are Christ's body, and individually parts of it.

Although the tenth chapter (verse 17) of the first letter to the Corinthians initially mentions the body ("we, though many, form one body"), the theme is not elaborated upon until the twelfth chapter. The text above is the largest "block" of Paul's thoughts on the body of Christ in all his writings. Although he mentioned the body elsewhere in other letters, in none of his writings is the concept so fully developed. Different aspects of his thought will be examined with specific verses, with the wisdom of various biblical scholars guiding us in this process.

According to Martin, 1 Corinthians is an example of a popular form of rhetorical speech called *homonoia* or harmony/unity exhortations,[1] and contains elements of those exhortations such as unity, mutual benefit or interdependence, and different functions serving the same goal.[2] "Paul's constant concern throughout the letter is the unity of the church, Christ's body. Many of the

---

1. Martin, *Corinthian Body*, 38.

2. Martin, *Corinthian Body*, 94.

terms Paul employs are borrowed directly from Greek *homonoia* speeches, and his rhetorical strategy of urging the Corinthians to do what is beneficial and what will make for the common advantage, rather than exercising their complete autonomy, is that of *homonoia* speeches."[3] "*Homonoia* speeches always assume that the body is hierarchically constituted and that illness or social disruption occurs when that hierarchy is disrupted, . . . [such as in] class conflict."[4] Although Paul used this rhetoric of unity, he did not do so to maintain the status quo (which *was* the purpose of *homonoia*), but to overturn it, as Martin and other scholars have noted. "Paul's insistence on an equal partnership of the higher- and lower-status entities would have been heard as a reversal of their statuses,"[5] or "[t]he lower is made higher, and the higher lower."[6]

Overall,

> "... the Body metaphor is for Paul an image of the Church which refers primarily to our common dependence on Christ, joint partaking of his Spirit, interdependence on one another, unity in Christ, and responsibility for mutual service .... what was determinative for Paul ... was the thought of believers' common, or rather collective, relationship to their Head, Christ ...."[7]

According to biblical scholar Michael Gorman:

> The reality of the diversity of gifts but unity of source (God) and purpose (edification of the community) creates a fundamental equality in the church, which Paul now addresses with the language of a 'body' .... [Paul's] image of the body conveys four interconnected main points, three conventional and one not. The conventional points are bodily unity in diversity (12:14, 20), the necessity of all parts (12:15–19, 21), and the solidarity, or mutual interdependence, of all parts (12:26). Feet, hands,

---

3. Martin, *Corinthian Body*, 39.

4. Martin, *Corinthian Body*, 40.

5. Martin, *Corinthian Body*, 102.

6. Martin, *Corinthian Body*, 96.

7. Cole, *Body of Christ*, 26.

ears, eyes, the nose—all are necessary; there can be no body without diverse bodily parts. So, too, Paul implies, the church consists of people with various backgrounds and gifts, all of whom are necessary for the activity of the body (12;19), and all of whom need one another and should care for one another (12:25–26). No one should feel inferior ("I'm not needed," 12:15–16) or superior ("you're not needed," 12:21). The unconventional point in 12:14–26 appears at this juncture . . . . Not only are feelings of inferiority or superiority inappropriate, but in the church the apparently "weaker" members are actually "indispensable," and the "less honorable . . . less respectable" ones are treated with greater honor and respect (12:22–24a). This is by divine arrangement (12:24b), just as Paul said in 1:26–31, and is intended to preempt dissension by counterculturally showering more attention on those of less status so that all will receive equal care (12:25). Moreover, when one member of the church suffers either ill or good fortune, the entire church stands with that member, irrespective of that member's status in worldly terms (12:25–26).[8]

Each of these four themes—unity in diversity (12:14, 20), necessity of all parts (12:15—19, 21), mutual interdependence (12:26), and the greater honor accorded to the weaker (12:22—24a)—will be examined individually.

Unity in diversity (12:14, 20)

(14) Now the body is not a single part, but many. (20) But as it is, there are many parts, yet one body.

Unity is a paramount principle for the human body and the body of Christ. The human body is not a collection of diverse parts with no relationship to one another, but a unity of millions and millions of diverse parts, all interacting with each other for the good of the entire body. In the human body, this unity is based on the common genetic material in each cell and, hence, in each

---

8. Gorman, *Apostle of the Crucified Lord*, 272–73.

organ. That is why a transplanted organ has a difficult time being accepted by its new body—it does not have the same genetic material as the rest of this body. In the body of Christ, it is Christ himself whose life (Spirit) permeates every member of his body, by their immersion in him. This creates the fundamental unity of the body of Christ: oneness with Christ and oneness among Christ's people. Unlike the very real possibility of rejection for a transplanted organ in the human body, a new (i.e., transplanted) member in the body of Christ is not rejected but, instead, receives the imprint of Christ through the sacraments of Baptism and Eucharist. Baptism introduces us into the body of Christ through the power of the Holy Spirit; Eucharist joins us intimately to Christ, for as we receive him, he nourishes us.

In *The Cost of Discipleship*, Lutheran pastor Dietrich Bonhoeffer commented:

> . . . baptism confers the privilege of participation in all the activities of the Body of Christ in every department of life. To allow a baptized brother to take part in the worship of the Church, but to refuse to have anything to do with him in everyday life, is to subject him to abuse and contempt. If we do that, we are guilty of the very Body of Christ. And if we grant the baptized brother the right to the gifts of salvation, but refuse him the gifts necessary to earthly life or knowingly leave him in material need or distress, we are holding up the gifts of salvation to ridicule and behaving as liars . . . . When a man is baptized into the Body of Christ, not only is his personal status as regards salvation changed, but also the relationship of daily life.[9]

Modern biblical scholars further underscore Paul's meaning.

"Just as the body has many limbs and organs and despite their number and differences make up one body, so Christ's body has many limbs and organs and despite their number and differences make up one body . . . . He [Paul] pictures the church not as a body

---

9. Bonhoeffer, *Cost of Discipleship*, 287.

of Christians but as the body of Christ. There is unity in plurality, but not uniformity."[10]

There is ". . . a mystical identification of all Christians with the body of Christ. . . . the body with which this mystical identification is made, is none other than [Christ] the real and personal body which lived, died, and was glorified, and with which the bread in the Eucharist is identified . . . ."[11] "There is only one life—that of Christ risen from the dead. There is only one body—the one that is animated by that life."[12] "The beloved Church of Christ is, after all, flesh-and-blood Christians, living Christian lives in this world."[13] Or, as Bonhoeffer put it, "The Body of Christ can only be a visible Body, or else it is not a Body at all."[14]

Without each member losing his or her individuality, the members receive a new spirit that unites them. "The community can be called Christ's body, because the individual bodies of community members contain the [external] spirit Paul identifies with Christ . . . . Paul asserts that the community of believers is united in a literal, though spiritual, way by the reception of the spirit of Christ into the individual body of each believer."[15] "[M]any bodies become one body, because they share *one* spirit."[16]

Reflection Questions

1. *Does the idea of being in union with many persons who are quite different racially, socially, politically, or economically from yourself energize you or give you pause?*

10. Garland, *1 Corinthians*, 590.
11. Cerfaux, *Church in the Theology of St. Paul*, 277–278.
12. Cerfaux, *Church in the Theology of St. Paul*, 368.
13. Cerfaux, *Church in the Theology of St. Paul*, 382.
14. Bonhoeffer, *Cost of Discipleship*, 277.
15. Hollingshead, *Household of Caesar and the Body of Christ*, 159.
16. Hollingshead, *Household of Caesar and the Body of Christ*, 166.

2. *In your own congregation, do you really feel as if you are in
   union with all of the other members? What might be preventing
   you from feeling this way?*

Necessity of all parts (12:15—19, 21)

**(15) If a foot should say, "Because I am not a hand, I do not
belong to the body," it does not for this reason belong any less to
the body. (16) Or if an ear should say, "because I am not an eye,
I do not belong to the body," it does not for this reason belong
any less to the body. (17) If the whole body were an eye, where
would the hearing be? If the whole body were hearing, where
would the sense of smell be? (18) But as it is, God placed the
parts, each one of them, in the body as he intended. (19) If they
were all one part, where would the body be? (21) The eye cannot
say to the hand, "I do not need you," nor the head to the feet, "I
do not need you."**

In the human body, all parts are necessary, regardless of how
unnecessary, on the surface, they seem to be; we are called to recognize and accept how God has fashioned the human body with
its great diversity of body parts. When one part of the body rejects
another part (e.g., an autoimmune disease), it rejects part of itself,
thus jeopardizing not only the health of that part, but the health—
and, perhaps, even the life—of the entire body. In the case of such
a physical disease, it is unclear why some parts of the body cannot
accept that the rejected body part truly belongs (i.e., has the same
genes as the rest) to them in an intimate way. So, too, with the body
of Christ: God has bestowed membership and various gifts so as
to build up the church, not for any one person's edification alone.
Thus, individuals are called to yield to the community, and that is
why it is so pointless and so tragic when members of a church (or
the church) are territorial or segregate themselves from others.

"Paul insists that a separatist or individualistic attitude by
one of the members of the body does not 'make it any less a part
of the body' (v.15). Body members cannot be reconstituted as

independent entities because 'God arranged the members in the body, each one of them, as he chose (v.18)."[17]

Paul certainly uses highly imaginative personifications of body parts in verses 15 through 21, but this was not unique to him. Thiselton noted that nearly a hundred years earlier, Dionysius of Halicarnassus (c. 30 BCE) personified parts of the body.[18] Fee noted, ". . . Paul begins with a personification of some of the parts of the body, in which they are disallowed to say things either about themselves (vv. 15–16) or about others (v. 21) because what is said is absurd in terms of the body . . . . that all members are necessary if there is to be a body and not a monstrosity."[19] ". . . if all were one part, other functions would be lacking . . . . The concern for diversity can scarcely be missed."[20] According to Garland:

> . . . Paul fancifully addresses the envy or disdain that one member of the body might have for another . . . . Both eyes and ears, hands and feet, have their assigned function in the body, without which the body becomes disabled. The failure of one little valve can shut down the whole bodily system. The implication is that there is no unimportant gift or person in the body of Christ.[21]

> In 12:17, Paul carries the whimsy further. What if the whole body were an eye? This freakish object would have no sense of smell, no faculty of hearing, no way to perambulate except to roll around, no way to feed itself or digest. A well functioning body requires a multiplicity of members with a multiplicity of functions . . . God made the body with its intricately interconnected parts so that it could perform at its optimum in this world.[22]

Thiselton also underscored this unity of purpose:

17. Horsley, *1 Corinthians*, 172.
18. Thiselton, *First Epistle to the Corinthians*, 992–993.
19. Fee, *First Epistle to the Corinthians*, 608–609.
20. Fee, *First Epistle to the Corinthians*, 611.
21. Garland, *1 Corinthians*, 594.
22. Garland, *1 Corinthians*, 595.

The respective functions of the hands, feet, (v. 15), ears, and eyes (v. 16) *coordinate* the body as one. If each did not play his or her assigned role, the one body would collapse into a chaotic nonentity. Hence, v. 15 not only reassures those who feel inferior that they do indeed belong to the body, but also asserts the necessity for the coherent unity of the body both of those who feel inferior and to those who devalue others . . . . [U]nless the many perform their assigned functions, however diverse, the one body would not exist as a single entity but as a chaotic array of conflicting forces, without focus or coherence."[23]

Although certain body parts seem nobler than other parts, it would be absurd to think that the entire body could function as a single body part, no matter how noble that part seems to be. In an extended section of his work, Thiselton addressed this issue.

To try to rank some gifts as "more essential" than others, let alone as necessary marks of advanced status to which all should aspire, is to offer a blasphemous challenge to God's freedom to choose whatever is his goodwill for his people both collectively and individually . . . . How dare anyone either boast or exult in his or her own gifts as if these were a status symbol, or devalue other people's gifts, as if God had not chosen them for the other?[24]

Not only does the rhetoric of the body reassure those with supposedly "inferior" or "dispensable" gifts that they do indeed belong fully to the body as essential limbs and organs, but *this rhetoric now explicitly rebukes those who think that they and their "superior" gifts are self-sufficient for the whole body, or that others are scarcely "authentic" parts of the body, as they themselves are.*[25]

Then and now, those who think that they are somehow special because of their gifts or roles might be tempted to consider themselves to be *the* most important members who safeguard the church's legacy. Thiselton cautioned:

23. Thiselton, *First Epistle to the Corinthians*, 1002.

24. Thiselton, *First Epistle to the Corinthians*, 1004.

25. Thiselton, *First Epistle to the Corinthians*, 1005.

> Those whom the church likes to put "on display" as our "best" people (whether because of their supposed wisdom and knowledge, or the more visible gifts of the Spirit (such as tongues or "mighty works") are far from being the essence of the church. These are those who are needy and know of their need . . . . Unlike status seekers "on display" in the church, who have absorbed the competitive spirit of secular Corinth, "the blessed [are those] refusing to be in tune with the world . . . ."[26]

> The obsession with groups and status *tears* and splits the body of Christ, limb from limb, organ from organ . . . . the *care* or concern . . . of a given individual or group should have been directed not at their own standing or role, but equally at the standing or role of the whole body.[27]

Banks noted that "each member of the community is granted a ministry to other members of the community."[28]

> The community contains a great diversity of ministries, and it is precisely in the difference of function that the wholeness and unity of the body resides . . . . This means that each member has a unique role to play, yet is also dependent upon everyone else. It is precisely those members who render the less obviously spectacular services who should be accorded the greatest respect. The most outwardly attractive or dramatic ministries are not necessarily the most fundamental . . . . [29]

Commenting on the Christian community throughout history, Haight noted:

> . . . many talents cooperate to make the Church a complex organic unity . . . . The Spirit of God who is the Spirit of Christ is the life blood of this identification, thus suggesting active participation in God . . . . [Paul's] image pointedly celebrates the pluralism and diversity of gifts,

26. Thiselton, *First Epistle to the Corinthians*, 1009.

27. Thiselton, *First Epistle to the Corinthians*, 1011.

28. Banks, *Paul's Idea of Community*, 63.

29. Banks, *Paul's Idea of Community*, 64.

and simultaneously insists that they constitute the unity
of the one body and have to be exercised toward that end
. . . . It bears more than a hint of egalitarianism: the different gifts correlate with different functions, some more
important than others, but all are members of the same
body . . . .[30]

Reflection Questions

1. *Does it seem reasonable to you that every person in the body of
   Christ has a role to play? How about in your own church?*

2. *Does it seem that the body might be better off without certain
   persons or with only certain others in positions of prominence?
   How about in your own church?*

Mutual interdependence (12:26)

**(26) If [one] part suffers, all the parts suffer with it; if one part
is honored, all the parts share its joy.**

Paul insisted that both unity and diversity are needed in any
body in order for its proper functioning. In a well-functioning
body, a body in which all parts work in harmony with each other,
one cannot have unity without diversity, nor diversity without an
inherent unity. In a disease such as cancer, the diversity remains,
but the unity is compromised as certain cells act as if they are completely independent, acting according to their own plan. In so doing, they jettison the "grand plan" for the body and risk its very life.

"Differences of status, hierarchies of power, or wisdom, or
knowledge, cannot be valued or even created in the community
that forms the body of Christ. Each member, each organ, each
limb, needs all the others."[31] Other scholars make similar points.

30. Haight, *Christian Community in History,* 117.

31. Hollingshead, *Household of Caesar and the Body of Christ,* 194.

> . . . if the ear and fingers of a musician are praised, or if the hands and feet of an athlete are praised, a person receives congratulations for his or her coordination as a whole. The whole person is described as a good musician or as a good athlete . . . . Those at Corinth who make others feel inferior merely to enhance their own status thus ultimately demean themselves, and Christ . . . ."[32]

In other words, gifts used well evoke joy; gifts ignored or used over and against others evoke pain and grief.

> Because God has arranged the body as an interdependent organism in which diversity is essential, the differences between the members should not lead to division . . . but to the members' caring for each other . . . . [Paul] envisions not just the tolerance of differences within the community but a gracious and compassionate synergy in which all members share one another's sorrows and joys (v. 26) . . . . everybody knows how a pain in the ankle or finger can absorb the entire body's energy and attention. That, Paul contends, is how things are in the church. He does not speak of what should be, but of what is: the body really is diminished and pained by the suffering of any of its members. The same principle applies to the honor shown any one member: the body really does celebrate it together . . . . The more obviously honorable members of the church should rejoice in showing honor to the less honorable.[33]

> [In verse 25] [t]he analogy is easily understood, especially the first part. It is difficult to study when one has a toothache; the whole body suffers with the part that is aching. More difficult is the second part, "if one part is honored, every part rejoices with it" . . . . one can see the net drawing closer around the Corinthians . . .[34]

It *is* difficult to extrapolate to human behavior the idea that when part of the body is praised, the whole body rejoices because

32. Thiselton, *First Epistle to the Corinthians*, 1012.

33. Hays, *First Corinthians*, 216.

34. Fee, *First Epistle to the Corinthians*, 615.

in human relationships, frequently the opposite is true: some might be envious over another's success or honor. Yet, that is not the way it should be. In solidarity, we are to rejoice with those who rejoice and mourn with those who mourn. Garland noted that long before the Letter to the Corinthians was written, Plato, in *Respublica* 5.10.462C–D, noted, "When one of us has a wounded finger, the body and soul of that person and their inter-relationship are affected, and we say *the man* feels pain in his finger. Even so with every other part of the body—when one part suffers there is pain, and there is joy when one part is restored to health."[35]

Although the individual has a dignity that is to be respected by the community, the community has a prominence that is to be acknowledged and respected by each individual. The beauty of the community is undergirded by the beauty of each individual, but the beauty is much deeper than a mere sum of the parts.

> The community at Corinth is not said to be *part* of a wider body of Christ nor as "*a* body of Christ" alongside numerous others. It is "*the* body of Christ" in that place.[36]

> ... [Paul] does not say that the experiences of individuals within the community, both pleasurable and sorrowful, *should* be shared by all the others who belong to it. He says instead that they *are* so shared, whether others consciously experience them or not. The "body" has a common nerve. There is a common life within it in which each is identified with the other—all in one, as it were, and one in all (v.26) .... The closeness of the relationship between the community and Christ is [thus] underlined ....[37]

> ... it is good that different individuals have different gifts, and all these different gifts must be orchestrated together for the common good of the community. ... Some churches, more susceptible to the error of "Lone Ranger" Christianity, may need to hear the appeal for

---

35. Garland, *1 Corinthians*, 598.

36. Banks, *Paul's Idea of Community*, 63.

37. Banks, *Paul's Idea of Community*, 64.

interdependence emphasized, while others, more inclined to press for conformity of Christian experience, may need to hear Paul's affirmation of diverse gifts within the body of Christ. In any case, the image of the body of Christ, as Paul has developed it, provides a vision for authentic community in which there is great individual freedom (vv. 14–20) and powerful interpersonal sharing and support (vv. 21–26). The goal of our ministry should be nothing less than the formation of such communities.[38]

Just as the goal, or the end, of each individual member of community is the common good of that larger community, so also the goal, or end, of each organ or muscle in our body is the common good of the overall person. The function of the liver, for example, is to reduce the level of toxic elements for the health of the overall body. But, the goal of the liver is the good of the person. Within the human body, the particular role of each organ works harmoniously, or at least is supposed to, to produce the common good of the body. So humans have their particular functions and goals within the wider society, but the ultimate goal of each of us is the good common to all of us . . . . The common good is not simply the sum total of each person's particular economic good, but is in reality the final goal of the individual person . . . . Consider again the analogy of the human body: the liver can only serve the body by exercising its particular function of reducing toxic elements, not by having some general non-specific function. The doctrine of the common good embodies a personalist approach in which we love our neighbor particularly, not merely humanity in general . . . . if we are caught up in ourselves, we will overlook the needy ones whose paths we cross everyday. To work for the common good requires that we help this particular person . . . . the goal of our individual lives is the good of the larger community in which we live. But the Body of

38. Hays, *First Corinthians*, 220.

Christ extends through all time and space so that we are joined with the saints of biblical and later times.[39]

This interdependence is true even when the pastor or other leader of the church is less gifted in some ways than are other members of the assembly. In what could be said about any church leader (ordained or lay, man or woman), Lusk in 2004 noted:

> After all, the ordained man [sic] is fallible. He will make mistakes, misspeak, and even sin. He is often inferior in intelligence and speaking ability to those who must learn from him. Many in the congregation will ordinarily excel the pastor in various ways. And yet all are expected to humbly receive God's truth from him . . . Christ cultivates humility and teachableness in the body by organizing it around a weak and frail representative of himself.[40]

> Faith needs more than book-learning to grow. Our faith is often challenged and nourished most by trials and triumphs, the tribulations and joys, of living in close-knit community. By rubbing shoulders with one another, iron sharpens iron. Sparks may fly from time to time, but the end result is that we are sharpened and our rough edges are smoothed over. By helping one another through good times and bad, we not only learn how to apply our storehouse of theological knowledge; we actually accumulate wisdom we could never garner out of academic Bible studies . . . . After all, God did not promise, "I will be your God, and you will be my *persons*." He said, "I will be your God, and you will be my *people*." And those people are bonded together by more than a creed. The tie that binds includes the mind, but goes to the heart.[41]

39. Dauphinais, "Common Good and the Body of Christ."

40. Lusk, "Calvin on Pastor and Community."

41. Lusk, "Calvin on Pastor and Community."

Reflection Questions

1. *What gifts do you have that the body of Christ needs, especially in your own church?*

2. *What do you lack that others in the body of Christ, especially in your own church, can provide for you?*

Greater honor accorded to the weaker (12:22–24)

(22) Indeed, the parts of the body that seem the weaker are all the more necessary, (23) and those parts of the body that we consider less honorable, we surround with greater honor, and our less presentable parts are treated with greater propriety, (24) whereas our more presentable parts do not need this. But God has so constructed the body as to give greater honor to a part that is without it . . . .

What are the weaker body organs to which Paul compares the more lowly members of the Corinthian church? Internal organs? Limbs that do all the work? Sexual organs? Scholars differ in their opinions, but all agree that Paul was making the point that all members of a body are important to that body, regardless of what cultural norms or our senses tell us otherwise. Looks can be deceiving; cultural norms can be tragically flawed or even death-dealing. ". . . the weakest members in the Christian community become the decisive criterion for the conduct of all. Even Christ is not the dominating part in the 'body of Christ.' He forms the entire body. He is just as present in the weakest members as in the strongest."[42]

> Both the direction and content of what is said imply a view "from above," where those who consider themselves at the top of the "hierarchy" of persons in the community suggest that they can get along without some of the others, who do not have their supposedly superior rank . . .

42. Thiessen, *Psychological Aspects of Pauline Theology*, 329.

the implication of the analogy as Paul proceeds with it is that some *people* consider themselves superior to others, not that some *gifts* are superior . . . .[43]

Appearances deceive, Paul is saying. If one removed an organ because it appeared weak, the body would cease to be whole. So with the church. All the parts are necessary, no matter what one may think.[44]

The high-status Corinthians may look down their noses at their uncouth lower-class brothers and sisters in the faith, regarding them as something of an embarrassment, but Paul insists that they must be "clothed" with dignity and honor . . . not only are they indispensable to the healthy functioning of the whole body, but God has arranged the body in such a way that greater honor is to be given to those who in the natural order of things might be despised (v.24).[45]

"Eye" and "head" are transparent metaphors for those in leadership roles, who are likely to be more affluent and better educated. The "hands" and the "feet" represent the laboring class or slaves. "Eyes" and "heads" in the church always get special treatment and then begin to think that they are special.[46]

"A sense of superiority can breed notions of self-sufficiency."[47] No body part is autonomous, and sometimes it is those body parts that we would not be interested in showing the world that are the most important in terms of our overall health. This is yet another example of how looks can be deceiving. After all, who shows off their kidneys or their lungs? Yet, without the proper functioning of these organs, toxins would accumulate in the body, and the person would likely die.

---

43. Fee, *First Epistle to the Corinthians*, 612.

44. Fee, *First Epistle to the Corinthians*, 613.

45. Hays, *First Corinthians*, 216.

46. Garland, *1ˢᵗ Corinthians*, 595.

47. Oster, *1 Corinthians*, 304, quoted in Garland, *1 Corinthians*, 595.

A body can survive without eyes, ears, hands, and feet, but it cannot survive without the function of these unpresentable parts. Genitalia appear to be honorless . . . . Their function is not public, and they are kept hidden, but they are essential to the body's survival. In the same manner, the persons with deceptively ordinary and unprestigious gifts are as necessary for the proper functioning of community as those who put on a more glittery display. All are of equal value; but if there is to be any overcompensation, it is to be for the less favored. The church is not to be like its surrounding society, which always honors those who are already honored. It is to be countercultural and bestow the greatest honor on those who seems negligible.[48]

Paul is not saying that a given individual in the community is "Christ's eye" and another is "Christ's foot." But he is observing that those parts of the human body which were deemed "unpresentable" were actually treated with greater care and modesty than those that were "presentable." The weaker were treated better than the stronger. *Because* the body of Christ is *also* a body, such should be the case with its members . . . . Differences within the community, in fact, are evidence that the members *are* a unity: "if all was one member, where would be the body?" . . . The body of Christ is a single body, a unity. Because of that, the creation of hierarchy within the community cannot be tolerated. God grants gifts and roles as *he* sees fit. These cannot be achieved through special rites or initiations, and they are not reasons to boast, for they have been received, and not earned. In fact, those with the seemingly greater gifts, those who are approved *by God*, use their gifts, their wisdom, their power, only for the community as a whole, and not for themselves. And this leads us to the other central concern of Paul's letters: weakness . . . . the more seemly members of the body are compelled to care for the less seemly; the powerful, the wise, and the knowledgeable must give honor to the

48. Garland, *1 Corinthians*, 596.

weak, the foolish, and the ignorant, because they are all members of the same whole.[49]

Why is this so? God chooses the weak of this world (1:27; 4:10; 9:22) to confound the supposedly strong or wise, who should share whatever "glory" they might possess instead of flaunting their status or "lording it over others," as Christ warned his disciples not to do (Matt 20:25). Webb-Mitchell wrote in *Christly Gestures*:

> . . . it is in the eyes of the marginalized that we experience the ways that we have participated in a system that has robbed people of justice, love, and hope in their lives. We may see in the eyes of the poor and disabled not only the weaknesses of others but also our own personal weaknesses. . . . [Christ] calls us to stop looking for the Holy Spirit everywhere else but in the eyes of those who are homeless or victims of rape, those in prison or in drug halfway houses . . . . Christ has no hands but our hands in reaching out to those who need assistance just as we need his hands when we feel fragile . . . The streets of our modern world make up one of the best classrooms for learning and performing gestures of charity, hospitality, courage, and justice, and for speaking the truth in love . . . in our gestures , God in Christ continues to be on the side of those who love and fear God in every generation, and God scatters the proud in their conceit while lifting up the lowly.[50]

Fee understood that this was not just a issue for the Corinthians but for all people. ". . . much of the tension in the [Corinthian] community is the result of social status . . . the apparently superior cannot say to the apparently inferior, 'We can get along without you' . . . the conclusion drawn is . . . the need for unity and mutual concern, with a decided emphasis on God's own care for the one who lacks."[51]

---

49. Hollingshead, *Household of Caesar and the Body of Christ*, 192–93.

50. Webb-Mitchell, *Christly Gestures*, 240–41.

51. Fee, *First Epistle to the Corinthians*, 609.

Compared with Aesop's fable about the belly and the rest of the body, Paul is less concerned that the lowly will rise up against the mighty than he is that the mighty will misuse their status. "His use of the body metaphor turns things upside down. Rather than urging the weak to stop their unruly behavior and to give due honor and respect to the strong,"[52] "[Paul] urges the strong (probably the well-to-do) to give more honor and respect to the weak, and so cease their fractious behavior."[53]

> . . . some members could go missing [at the Lord's Supper] with no great loss to the church [i.e., the other members]. All have experienced, at one time or another, how the whole physical body suffers when one member hurts. The same is true for the body of Christ. As one attends to physical ailments in the body, so Paul expects the church to attend to those who are suffering. The principle of love embodied in the cross mandates that one should always seek honor for others, which stands in absolute antithesis to the dominant value that seek honor only for oneself in preening self-indulgence.[54]

"The apparently 'higher' members (eyes and head) cannot scorn the hands and feet, without whom they would have no power to act (vv. 21–22); likewise, the different members of the church need one another."[55]

> "Paul is writing to correct the behavior of some haughty Corinthians whose undisciplined flaunting of spiritual gifts has caused the weaker and less honorable members of the community (vv. 22–23) to feel despised and even ostracized from the body because they do not have the same exalted spiritual experiences (vv. 15–16) . . . . Seeking to overcome this sad division (*schisma* 12:25) in the church, Paul calls upon all Corinthians to see themselves joined together as members of one body with a stake in one another's peace and wellbeing. This message makes

52. Garland, *1 Corinthians*, 594.

53. Witherington, *Conflict and Community in Corinth*, 254.

54. Garland, *1 Corinthians*, 597.

55. Hays, *First Corinthians*, 215.

particular demands on those who hold the upper roles in the social structure and upon those who receive the most impressive spiritual gifts . . . . A conversion of the imagination will be necessary for those in a position of privilege truly to see themselves as bound together with the weaker members of the body. Such a conversion is the aim of Paul's letter and it should be the aim of our teaching and preaching as well.[56]

The so-called weak must not feel that if they happen not to have received certain gifts, they are somehow not a genuine part of the body . . . . Paul reassures those who are anxious about comparisons with supposedly more "gifted" members, and underlines their role, status, and welcome. On the other side, he rebukes the "strong" who seem to think that only those of similar social status and similar spiritual gifts are "real" Christians.[57]

. . . the spiritual gifts of others are to be recognized, accepted, and affirmed (12:14–26), with special, even exaggerated consideration given to the "weaker" or less prominent members of the body and their gifts (12:22–26).[58]

Although there is a hierarchy to the gifts, based on their perceived ability to benefit the community (1 Cor 12:28; chp 14), everyone possesses a gift, and each gift—and therefore each member of the community—is important and valued. Indeed, the socially inferior are the communally superior; status is not only transcended but reversed . . . .[59]

Then as now, all of "us" have been given gifts that complement each other and serve—if used rightly—to build up the body of Christ and, in doing so, encounter the living God in the faces of each other. Gifts are received by the recipient and not invented or created by her or him. As such, how can any of us think more

56. Hays, *First Corinthians*, 220.

57. Thiselton, *First Epistle to the Corinthians*, 990.

58. Gorman, *Cruciformity*, 236.

59. Gorman, *Cruciformity*, 300–301.

of ourselves about any gift, especially since it is meant to be used for the benefit of more than its recipient? Each gift is, to use Webb-Mitchell's term, a "social gift."[60] Webb-Mitchell quoted Thomas Aquinas, writing, "Diversity of states and functions in the church doesn't hinder its unity; indeed that is rather perfected by faith, love, and mutual ministry to one another . . . . So diversity among the members of the church contributes to its perfection, its effective function, and its beauty."[61]

As Gorman noted, gifts are to be recognized and acknowledged by both the individual and his or her faith community, and even if we are unimpressed by the recipient of the gift, we are to honor him or her and the giftedness. "Instead, it was—and is—God's intention to lift up those who have been relegated to the fringes by others more powerful, even in the church today. God instills in them a heart for justice where there is injustice; peace where there is violence; and love where there is hatred."[62] "Each person, regardless of his or her capajcity or limitations intellectually, physically, emotionally, or spiritually is blessed by God in Christ with such gifts for the common good and further up-building of Christ's Body."[63] Webb-Mitchell evokes Yoder saying, in other words, each person—no matter how flawed or limited—is irreplaceable, for any member "can be crippled through no fault of its own when some other part of the body suffers."[64]

Reflection Questions

1. *Whom would you call the weaker members of your local church congregation? Why are they "weaker" or "less honorable"? How are they treated by others?*

60. Webb-Mitchell, *Christly Gestures*, 61.
61. Webb-Mitchell, *Christly Gestures*, 70.
62. Webb-Mitchell, *Christly Gestures*, 61.
63. Webb-Mitchell, *Christly Gestures*, 233–34.
64. Webb-Mitchell, *Christly Gestures*, 66.

2. *Who are the "more presentable" members of your congregation? How do they treat members who are not like them?*

3. *Into which category do you place yourself?*

Summary

> [In verse 27] Paul returns to the opening affirmation about the body of Christ. In case the Corinthians have not realized it, he clarifies that he is talking about them. They are Christ's body . . . . Everybody relates to Christ and to one another as a part of his body. As "parts," each has his or her own function that contributes to the body's welfare. Again, Paul focuses on God as the one who orchestrates the gifts in the church (12:6, 18, 24) in the same way that God arranged the intricacies of the body.[65]

Just as the head rules the human body, so too does Christ rule his body of believers, not from far away but even closer than the human head is to the rest of its body, for he is one with his members. In this, there is one body (composed of many members) and one life, shared by all, and animated by the Holy Spirit. As members of his body, we are completely dependent on him. Just as individual parts of a human body can do little (if anything) when separated from that body, so, too, we can do little when separated from Christ.

THE CHURCHES AT ROME AND EPHESUS

Although mention is made of "the body" in other letters, none have as complete an explanation as does 1 Corinthians. Mention here will be made to two other references: in Romans (written about 55–56 CE) and Ephesians (written about 63 CE).

---

65. Garland, *1 Corinthians*, 598.

Romans

The text is as follows:

Romans 12:4–6—(4) **For as in one body, we have many parts, and all the parts do not have the same function, (5) so we, though many, are one body in Christ and individually parts of one another.** (6) Since we have gifts that differ according to the grace given us, let us exercise them.

Bartlett noted that Paul meant no mere simile:

> When Paul writes in this way, he does not mean that the church is *like* Christ's body. He means the church *is* Christ's body . . . . That is very hard for us to grasp and harder for us to evade . . . . we are not only Christ's servants or Christ's followers: we *are* Christ's members, to one another and to the world outside as well . . . . Together we are Christ's body, but one by one we are only members of the body, and therefore need one another in order to be who we are, in order to be Christ.[66]

Again, in the letter to the Roman church, Paul stresses the unity-in-diversity theme: one body composed of many parts with differing functions. Yet, "though many," they are "one body in Christ," and, they are parts of each other. The obvious implication is that we would be foolish to shun parts of ourselves because, in doing so, we would only hurt ourselves. The gifts that are given are not a reason for envy or gloating but for celebrating and using them to build up the body. ". . . the church as Christ's body is not a motley aggregate of organs, but a living organism, some of whose organs are more important than others . . . . 'In Christ' this diversity is not something to be overcome but to be treasured and actualized rightly."[67]

Yet, we tend to lionize certain gifts or offices.

> We pretend that there are super Christians (often called clergy) and regular Christians. We pretend that . . . officeholders are obviously more valuable than those who

---

66. Bartlett, *Romans*, 112–13.

67. Keck, *Romans*, 298.

have no office . . . . We are called to be transformed . . .
when we are made new, we shall see how much we need
one another, how much we belong to one another, how
little ground we have for boasting . . . . Being the body of
Christ also means direct, practical care for one another.[68]

Instead of envying the gifts of others, we should concentrate
on using our own gifts to the best of our ability, using them more
for the benefit of the believing community than for private gain.
That requires a certain degree of maturity in that it is natural for
us to want what we do not have or to use what we have only for
ourselves in a type of scarcity mentality. Within the body of Christ,
focusing on others' gifts while ignoring—or even despising—our
own, cheats the body of the gifts we should be able to contribute.
As a consequence, the body is a bit poorer because we usurped
others' gifts and discounted our own.

Regardless of the gifts we have been given, we should not
think too highly (or lowly) of ourselves. God has given the gifts in
the way God has chosen for the benefit of the whole body, and it is
not up to any one person to second-guess God's choices. In today's
popular language, "it's not about us." Everything that is given is
done for the benefit of the *whole,* although, certainly, an individual
might benefit from his or her gifts exercised rightly.

Each person must accept God's grace to accept his or her
gift(s) *as they are,* without regarding them with grandiosity or
(alternatively) with disdain. "God's gifts are not given for the self-
congratulation of those who receive them, but for employment
in the building up of the body."[69] God's grace will ensure that the
body optimally functions, as each individual employs his or her
unique and diverse gifts, and is transformed in the process.

Understanding that Christians belong to one another in
one body and have in common the same grace of God (v.
5) and faith (vv. 3, 6) will help to stifle exaggerated ideas
about one's own status or ministry. And recognition of
the significant contribution made by each member of the

68. Bartlett, *Romans,* 114.

69. Barrett, *Romans,* 218.

> body of Christ will prevent one from thinking too highly (or too lowly) of him- or herself . . . . Paul is especially concerned that believers not take too individualistic an approach to transformation. Thus he wants us to recognize that the transformation of character is seen especially in our relationships with one another.[70]

> Paul . . . is exhorting each member of the community to use his or her gifts diligently and faithfully to strengthen the body's unity and help it to flourish.[71]

Ephesians

The texts are as follows:

Ephesians 1:22—And he put all things beneath his feet and gave him as head over all thing to **the church, which is his body,** the fullness of the one who fills all things in every way.

Ephesians 4:1–7; 11–13; 15–16—(1) I, then, a prisoner for the Lord, urge you to live in a manner worthy of the call you have received, (2) with all humility and gentleness, with patience, bearing with one another through love, (3) striving to preserve the unity of the spirit through the bond of peace: **(4) one body and one Spirit,** . . . (5) one Lord, one faith, one baptism; (6) one God and Father of all, who is over all and through all and in all. (7) But grace was given to each of us according to the measure of Christ's gift . . . (11) And he gave some as apostles, others as prophets, others as evangelists, others as pastors and teachers, (12) to equip the holy ones for the work of ministry, for **building up the body of Christ,** (13) until we all attain the unity of faith and knowledge of the Son of God, to mature manhood, to the extent of the full stature of Christ . . . (15) Rather, living the truth in love, we should grow in every way into him who is **the head, Christ, (16) from whom the whole body, joined and held together by every supporting ligament, with the**

---

70. Moo, *The Epistle to the Romans*, 758–59.
71. Moo, *The Epistle to the Romans*, 764.

proper functioning of each part, brings about the body's growth and builds itself up in love.

Ephesians 5:29–30—(29) No one heats his own flesh but rather nourishes it and cherishes it, even as Christ does **the church, (30) because we are members of his body**.

Again, Paul is making the connection between the church and the body of Christ, going so far as to say that the church *is* Christ's body. Our gifts are for the building up of the body (4:12) so that it becomes a mature person ". . . a corporate entity . . . . the community as a whole is growing into Christ—attaining the measure of the stature of the fullness of Christ."[72] In this body, Christ is the head, and the different ministries listed in verse 11 might be the "ligaments" to connect the various parts of the body with each other for optimal functioning and growth.[73] The balance that is required for this to happen has been ordained by God and the gifts God has given each person, which is Paul's constant theme across several letters. In loving each other and respecting each other's gifts (including one's own), the body continues to grow.[74]

Reflection Questions

1. *Unity, diversity of gifts, interdependence, and preferential treatment of the weakest—which of these four marks of Paul's vision of the body of Christ do you find most uplifting?*

2. *Which of these four marks is the most difficult for you to accept?*

3. *What do you think is your biggest challenge in embracing these concepts? Is it a larger challenge with regard to your local body of Christ or the universal body of Christ? What can you do to overcome those challenges?*

72. MacDonald, *Colossians and Ephesians*, 293.
73. MacDonald, *Colossians and Ephesians*, 295.
74. MacDonald, *Colossians and Ephesians*, 295.

A Final Word

Unity, diversity of gifts, interdependence, and preferential treatment of the weakest are all highlights of Paul's belief about the body of Christ. For Paul, this was no pious metaphor but a vibrant reality of believers' intimacy with Christ and with each other, brought about by God the Father who ordained the gifts of each member and the Holy Spirit's constant efforts to build up the body of Christ.

In our own churches, our own miniature bodies of Christ, how do these themes play out? Is our parish more like the congregation at Corinth than we'd like to admit? Or is it truly more in-tune with the ways of Christ? Is the church leadership enlivened by the notion of interdependence, or is it more interested in certain people calling the shots?

Perhaps, the more difficult questions are those we ask of ourselves: how do we as individuals see our roles in the body of Christ? Are we frequently envious of others' gifts or roles in our local church? Do we disparage them or refuse to cooperate? Or, do we discount our own gifts or even refuse to acknowledge them (let alone actualize them)? Do we want to be one of the "in" crowd or the highly visible group at church, or are we content to exercise our gifts and play our role in the background? After all, not every gift needs to be exercised with an audience present. Do we really feel that we are one with our fellow parishioners, delighted to be part of Christ's larger project? Or do we find ourselves resenting many of our fellow church members and their gifts or ideas? Do we really want to take the lead, or do we want Christ to be the lead?

Let us think about these questions and our relationship to our local body of Christ. For, if we cannot come to terms with God's plan in our own body of Christ, how will we come to terms with God's plan for the entire body of Christ that extends throughout the world, a plan that might relegate us to a even more subordinate position?

Chapter 3

The Development of the Doctrine of the Body of Christ as Community

WITH THE BACKGROUND ON Paul's use of the body theme for the church at Corinth and for the church for all ages, we are now in a position to examine the developing understanding of body of Christ theme. Because so many church leaders had something to say about this theme, only a representative three can be included in this chapter because of space. The Appendix contains additional material from early church leaders.

Since the emphasis in this text is on the interaction of one member of the body of Christ with others, the words of three Christian leaders will be highlighted: John Chrysostom (347–407 CE), Augustine (354–440 CE), and John Calvin (1509–1564). In addition, a teaching from the Second Vatican Council, as well as the writings of Pius Parcsh, a twentieth-century Catholic liturgist, who wrote one of the few books entirely on the body of Christ as community in the last century, will be included.

JOHN CHRYSOSTOM OF CONSTANTINOPLE

John Chrysostom (347–407 CE), archbishop of Constantinople, was one of the most eloquent preachers of his time or any time in the Christian tradition; his preaching was vibrant but also earthy, practical, and pithy. Unlike some of the other church fathers who have been quoted who were more cerebral, Chrysostom's gift was in getting the points across to those who listened to his sermons in churches. Portions of sermons that refer to the body of Christ as community follow, as quoted by various authors.

On the truth that we are many and diverse but one:

> When we communicate [i.e., receive communion] we do not simply receive a part, but we are united with Christ .... For what is the bread? It is the body of Christ. And what do the communicants become? The body of Christ. Not many bodies, but one body. For as the bread consists of many grains, so united that they are no longer distinguishable, and as they still subsist, though their individuality is no longer apparent to the eye because of their intimate union, so are we united with the other and with Christ .... If therefore by eating of the same body we all become that body, why do we not manifest to one another the same charity, and become one in this respect as well?[1]

On the reality of different gifts:

> Let us not envy those who have the higher gifts or look down on those who have the lesser ones, for this is the will of God. Let us not fight against him. And if you are still upset, understand that it is often the case that another cannot do what you can. Therefore, even if you are not

1. Mersch, *Whole Christ,* 327.

as great, you are superior in this; and even if someone is greater in certain things, he is not as great as you are in what you can do. Thus, there is equality. For in a body, too, the small parts make no small contribution, and their removal often harms the greater parts. What part of the body could be less important than hair? But remove this small thing from the eyebrows and the eyelids, and you destroy the beauty of the entire face, and the eyes no longer appear lovely . . . .[2]

On the physical body's concern for each member and how that should translate to the body of Christ:

But members [of the body of Christ] are bound to each other . . . by experiences, both pleasant and painful. Often when a thorn has pierced the heel, the whole body feels it and becomes concerned. The back bends over, the abdomen and legs join in, the hands . . . remove the thorn, the head bows down, and the eyes look on with great concern. As a result, even if the foot is at a disadvantage because it cannot raise itself up, it is made equal by the lowering of the head and enjoys equal honor . . . . Again, if something happens to the eyes, all the members feel pain, all are made idle. The feet do not walk or the hands work, and the stomach does not enjoy its usual foods. Yet the ailment belongs to the eye. Why does the stomach waste away? Why are your feet constrained? Why are your hands fettered? Because they are all bound up with the eyes, and the whole body suffers more than it can say . . . . [When] the head is crowned, the whole person is honored. The mouth speaks, and the eyes laugh with happiness, even though the credit does not belong to the beauty of the eyes but to the tongue . . . . [Let us not, then, exult] in the misfortunes of our neighbor, or envy his good fortune. This would be to act like a madman. For to gouge out one's own eye or devour one's own hand is undeniable evidence of insanity . . . . Tell me, why

2. Kovacs, *1 Corinthians*, 207–208.

> are you envious? Because your brother received some spiritual gift? And from whom did he receive it, pray tell? Was it not from God? Therefore, in envying, you make yourself an enemy of the one who gave the gift . . . .[3]

Unlike many early church fathers who concentrated on Christ's relationship to the members of his body rather than the members' relationship to each other, Chrysostom was particularly interested in how the members treated each other. For example, Chrysostom was particularly interested in Christ's identification with the poor.

> But we refuse to feed Him when He is hungry, to clothe Him when He is naked; when He asks an alms of us, we pass Him by. Oh, no doubt, if you were to see Christ Himself you would each give lavishly. But this man is Christ . . . . Why then do you not give Him all you have? . . . Whether you give to Him or to this beggar matters not, . . . To feed the Lord when He is visibly present, and when the very sight of Him would move a heart of stone, is not as meritorious as to care for the poor, the lame, and the deformed . . . . He it is whom we despise in the poor; hence the enormity of the crime . . . . Even though it be not Christ that we see, still, beneath these appearances it is really He who begs and receives. Do you blush at my saying that Christ begs? Blush rather with shame when He begs and you give not . . . ."[4]

Chrysostom must have shocked his listeners by reminding them that the poor and downtrodden were doing *them* a great favor (and not vice versa). "No surgeon, extending his hand and applying his knife, removes the festering parts of the wounds as well as a poor man who, by extending his right hand and receiving alms, relieves you of the scars left by your wounds. And the amazing thing is that the poor performs this salutary operation without causing pain or discomfort."[5]

3. Kovacs, *1 Corinthians*, 209–10.

4. Mersch, *Whole Christ*, 330–31.

5. Kovacs, *1 Corinthians*, 208.

Furthermore, he raged against excesses of church leaders that honored *things* but ignored *people*.

> What is the use of loading Christ's table with vessels of gold, if He Himself is dying of hunger? First satisfy His hunger; then adorn His table with what remains . . . . if you saw [a man] clothed in rags and shivering with cold, but without giving any thought to his raiment, you were to erect columns of gold, telling him that all this was in his honor, would he not think that you were mocking him and treating him with the utmost of contempt? But . . . this is the way you treat Christ . . . when instead of taking him in, you . . . suspend lamps from silver chains, but refuse to visit Him when He is in chains . . . . we must attend to both, but to Christ first![6]

> All this leaves us unmoved; so ungrateful are we that we deck out our servants, our mules, and our horses with trappings of gold, and despise our Lord who goes naked and begging from door to door and who stands with outstretched hand at the street corner. Nay, we often look at Him with distrust . . . . Your very dog is gorged with food, while Christ faints from hunger![7]

> . . . thou wilt not give even a bit of bread to Him . . . thou dost spurn Him when He is fainting from hunger, though everything you have . . . . He was not content merely to endure the cross and death; He willed to become a poor pilgrim, a beggar; He willed to be naked, to be cast into prison and to be subject to infirmities in order that these might at least move thy heart . . . .[8]

Comparing the altar of sacrifice (of the Eucharist) with the altar of the poor, one can perceive the passionate anger in Chrysostom.

> This stone altar is august because of the Victim that rests upon it; but the altar of almsgiving is more so because it

---

6. Mersch, *Whole Christ*, 331–32.

7. Mersch, *Whole Christ*, 332.

8. Mersch, *Whole Christ*, 333.

is made of this very Victim. The former is august because
. . . . it is sanctified by contact with the body of Christ;
the latter, because it is the body of Christ . . . . Thou dost
honor this altar because it receives the body of Christ.
But the other, which is the body of Christ, you treat with
ignominy and you look on indifferently while it perishes.
This altar you can see everywhere, in the streets and
in the market place, and at any hour you may sacrifice
thereon . . . .[9]

We ignore those with whom Christ most closely identifies,
while focusing our gaze on that which Christ never knew in his
lifetime. In words that can indict us in our own time, Chrysostom
imagined Christ sadly saying:

I ask thee for nothing costly, but for bread, a roof, and
words of comfort . . . . show at least a natural compassion when thou dost seest Me naked, and remember the
nakedness I endured for thee on the cross . . . . I was
thirsty as I hung on the cross, and I still thirst in the poor,
thus to draw thee to Myself . . . . Wherefore after having
bestowed a thousand favors upon thee, I ask thee some
return. I do so, not as demanding the repayment of a
debt, but that I may crown thy generosity . . . . I do not
say, "deliver Me from poverty" . . . . I ask only for bread,
for clothing, and for some little relief from My hunger.
If I am cast into prison, I do not ask that thou break My
bonds and set Me free; I ask only that thou come and see
Me who am in chains for thee . . . . This is why, though I
could feed Myself, I go begging; this is why I stand with
outstretched hand at thy door. I wish to be fed by thee,
for I love thee ardently. Like all who love, I am happy to
be at thy table. I am proud to be there, and I shall pro-
claim thee before the whole world, "Behold him who fed
Me."[10]

As an aside, Chrysostom undoubtedly knew that, centuries
earlier, the Christian apologist Tertullian (155–230 CE) had also

9. Mersch, *Whole Christ*, 335.
10. Mersch, *Whole Christ*, 334.

highlighted the need to treat others as if they were Christ, because, in some manner, they are. Tertullian wrote:

> Why dost thou look upon them [other persons] as different from thyself? . . . The body cannot take pleasure in the pain of one of its members; the whole body must needs suffer with it, and seek a remedy . . . . Therefore, when thou dost cast thyself at the knees of thy brethren, it is Christ whom thou dost embrace; it is Christ to whom thou dost pray. In like manner, when they lament over thee, it is Christ that mourns . . . .[11]

Reflection Questions

1. *Which of Chrysostom's concepts take you by surprise? Why?*

2. *What is most appealing about his viewpoint?*

3. *What do you make of his words, "What is the use of loading Christ's table with vessels of gold, if He Himself is dying of hunger? First satisfy His hunger; then adorn His table with what remains . . ." "All this leaves us unmoved; so ungrateful are we that we deck out our servants, our mules, and our horses with trappings of gold, and despise our Lord who goes naked and begging from door to door and who stands with outstretched hand at the street corner. Nay, we often look at Him with distrust . . . . Your very dog is gorged with food, while Christ faints from hunger!" How do these words apply today?*

AUGUSTINE OF HIPPO

Augustine of Hippo (354–440 CE) is one of the greatest saints in the Christian tradition. His rather wild life as a youth brought him no satisfaction, but his dedication to Christ after his well-known conversion (as described in his classic *Confessions*) brought him the peace for which he was longing. Although he dabbled in many

---

11. Mersch, *Whole Christ*, 372–73.

pagan ideas (and a few heresies) in his lifetime, his transformation after his conversion made him a most devoted follower of Christ. Indeed, it was his keen intellect that made him the great champion of the body of Christ by developing a more systematic theology of the body than had any of his predecessors. He did this, in part, to defend the faith against the heretics of his time; examples of his arguments against various heresies are found in the Appendix.

Throughout his ministry, Augustine systematically developed the ideas of (a) unity of Christ and members, (b) the importance of the Eucharist to strengthen the members and draw them more closely to Christ, (c) the importance of different roles or functions, (d) sharing of both joys and sorrows, (e) the necessity of suffering, and (f) the necessity of love of God and mutual love and service of members for each other. A brilliant homilist, Augustine expressed many of these thoughts about the body of Christ in sermons. In this section, emphasis is placed on items c through f.

Function

Like Paul, Augustine believed that each member of the body has his or her own important function. If each person does not do his or her part, the body cannot be what it was completely meant to be. If parts are at odds with each other, the body cannot function optimally.

> For as the members are formed singly and each has its particular function, and yet all live in the unity of the body; as the hand does what the eye cannot do, and as the ear can do what neither eye nor hand can do, yet all work together in unity, and as, though hand and eye and ear have different functions there is no discord between them, so it is in the body of Christ. Each man, as an individual member, has his own proper gifts, since He who chose people for His inheritance has fashioned their hearts one by one . . . . And just as in our members there is diversity of functions but unity of strength, so in all

Christ's members there is diversity of graces, but one charity.[12]

Sharing of Joys and Sorrows

The unity of Christ and his people [members] is so profound that all joys and sorrows *are* shared in a real way, just as it is in the human body, where the proper (or optimal) functioning of one organ is communicated to the others, and hence to the entire body. This is true even if two organs are not contiguous to each other. Likewise, in the body of Christ, when one member functions optimally by unselfish charity, members far away can experience that goodness. Augustine makes this point with an earthy example.

> Take an example from your body: your left hand has a ring on it . . . and your right hand has none. Does the right remain without adornment? If you look at the hands individually, you will see that one has adornment and the other doesn't. But if you look at the whole body to which the two hands are attached, you will see that the hand that lacks adornment possesses it in the hand that has it. The eyes can see where to walk and the feet walk where the eyes see. The feet cannot see, the eyes cannot walk. But the feet reply to you: "I too have light, not in me but in the eye. The eye does not see for its own sake without seeing for mine." The eyes also say: "We too walk, not in ourselves but in the feet. The feet do not carry themselves without carrying us . . . . if anything unpleasant happens to any member of the body, will any member refuse to come to its aid? What is remote from the center as the foot? And in the foot, what is as remote as the sole? And in the sole, what is as remote as the skin by which we touch the earth? But this remote member belongs to the body as a whole in such a way that if the sole treads on a thorn, the other members rush together to help remove it: immediately the knees bend, the spine curves over, and you sit down to pull out the thorn. The sitting to do

12. Mersch, *Whole Christ*, 429.

this belongs to the whole body. What a small spot is in trouble! The place that a thorn can puncture is tiny. And yet the pain felt in the tiny place is not left alone by the whole body; the other members feel no pain themselves, yet all feel pain in that place . . . . There is nothing higher and more honored in the body than the eyes. And nothing more remote than the little toe. Though that is so, it is better to be a toe in the body and enjoy health than to be an eye and to be inflamed and bleary. Health, which is common to all the members, is more valuable than the functions of them individually . . . . Whatever is diseased causes pain to the rest of the body. All the members make an effort to heal what is sick, and usually it is healed . . . . A member can admit health into itself only so long as it is not cut off from the body. Health flows from the other parts, which are sound, to the wounded place. But when the wounded part is cut off, there is no way for health to reach it.[13]

Suffering

The reality of the world is that there is suffering, and the members of Christ's body are not immune or shielded from it. Christ understands suffering in an intimate way because of his own experience as Jesus of Nazareth and continues to suffer as long as any of his members do.

"Christ's whole body groans in pain . . . . And each one of us has a part in the cry of that whole body . . . . The body of Christ ceases not to cry out all the day, one member replacing the other whose voice is hushed. Thus there is but one man who reaches unto the end of time, and those that cry are always His members."[14]

If one person suffers, then all do; that is what it means to be incorporated into Christ's body. We are called to suffer in solidarity with those joined to us in Christ, just as Christ suffers in solidarity with us. Augustine imagines Christ saying:

13. Kovacs, *1 Corinthians*, 212–13.
14. Mersch, *Whole Christ*, 423.

> "Thou art troubled today," He says, "and it is I that am
> troubled. Tomorrow another is troubled, again it is I
> that am troubled. After this generation will come others
> and yet others. They will be troubled, and it is I that am
> troubled. Until the end of time, whenever anyone in My
> body is in tribulation, it is I that am in tribulation" . . . .
> Christ is still suffering, not in His own flesh which He
> took with Him into heaven, but in my flesh, which is still
> suffering on earth.[15]

Furthermore, Augustine believes that, in some way, the sufferings of the members of the body are meant to complete Christ's
suffering. This notion might seem very outrageous to us: how
could any of us add to what Christ has done for humanity? But,
if we are truly one with Christ, he shares our sufferings, making
them his own. Who would deny that Christ's people continue to
suffer today? Who would deny that Christ's people—members of
his body—continue to be vilified and hated in our modern world?
Hence, Christ continues to experience suffering and vilification as
long as any of us do because he is united with us.

> . . . whatever you suffer at the hands of those who are not
> among the members of Christ, was lacking to the suffer-
> ings of Christ . . . . You fill up the measure, you do not
> cause it to overflow. You will suffer just so much as must
> be added of your sufferings to the complete passion of
> Christ, who suffered as our Head and who continues to
> suffer in His members, that is, in us. Into this common
> treasury each pays what he owes, and according to each
> one's ability we all contribute our share of suffering. The
> full measure of the Passion will not be attained until the
> end of the world. . . . All that occurred on the Cross . . . .
> happened in such a way as to prefigure, not in mysterious
> words only, but in a very reality, the Christian life that we
> are leading today.[16]

15. Mersch, *Whole Christ*, 424.
16. Mersch, *Whole Christ*, 425–426.

Mutual Love and Service

We are called to love and revere Christ. Loving Christ is not just loving the historical Jesus. It is loving his whole body, Christ and *all* his members wherever they may be. That love is actualized in charity and service.

> Extend thy charity over the entire earth if thou wilt love Christ, for the members of Christ are to be found everywhere in the world. If thou lovest only a part, thou art divided; if thou art divided, thou art not in the body; if thou art not in the body, thou art not under the Head. What is the use of believing, if thou dost blaspheme? Thou adorest Him as Head, and dost blaspheme Him in His body. He loves His body. Thou canst cut thyself off from the body, but the Head does not detach itself from its body. "Thou dost honor Me in vain," He cries from heaven, "thou dost honor Me in vain!" If someone wished to kiss thy cheek, but insisted at the same time on trampling thy feet; if with his nailed boots he were to crush thy feet as he tries to hold thy head and kiss thee, wouldst thou not interrupt his expressions of respect and cry out: "What art thou doing, man?" . . . [Christ] foresaw that many would pay Him homage because of His glory in heaven, but that their homage would be in vain, so long as they despise His members on earth."[17]

Augustine urges his listeners to love all people, even their enemies, just as Christ taught. If we only love certain persons, we do not truly love Christ, because Christ cannot be divided. Just as the Father cannot love only part of the Son, neither can we love only part of Him.

> Love all men, even your enemies; love them, not because they are your brothers, but that they may become your brothers . . . . Even he that does not as yet believe in Christ . . . love him, and love him with fraternal love . . . .

17. Mersch, *Whole Christ*, 436–37.

> Thus all our charity is brotherly love, and includes all the members of Christ.[18]

> And by loving he too becomes a member; through love he enters into the unity of the body of Christ, and there shall be one Christ loving Himself . . . . For when the members love one another, the body loves itself.[19]

> But when thou lovest thy brother, perhaps thou lovest him alone, but not Christ? . . . when thou lovest the members of Christ, it is Christ that thou lovest; in loving Christ, thou lovest the Son of God; in loving the Son of God, thou lovest the Father. Therefore love cannot be divided . . . . If thou lovest the Head, thou lovest also the members; if thou lovest not the members, neither dost thou love the Head.[20]

In *Sermon 137, 1*, Augustine noted that even when a member grows ill or weak in charity, he should not be cut off from the body, because once cut off, there is no chance of healing. The same is true in the human body. If a body part is ailing, cutting it off will not heal it but only serve to sever it from the body, effectively destroying it.

> Our Lord Jesus Christ . . . is the Head of the Church, and the Church is His body, and in his body it is the unity of the members and the union of charity that constitute its health, so that whenever a person grows cold in charity, he becomes a sick member of the body of Christ. But he who is our exalted head is also able to heal our infirm members, provided only they have not been cut off by undue weakness, but have adhered to the body until they were healed. For whatever still adheres to the body is not without hope of healing, but if he should be cut off from the body, his cure is impossible.[21]

18. Mersch, *Whole Christ*, 436.
19. Mersch, *Whole Christ*, 437.
20. Mersch, *Whole Christ*, 438.
21. Myers, "Mystical Body of Christ," XIX, §2, #4.

Reflection Questions

1. *Which of Augustine's concepts particularly appeals to you? Why?*

2. *What surprised you about Augustine's words?*

3. *What do you make of his words about the Eucharist, "'The Body of Christ' and you answer 'Amen.' Be therefore members of Christ that your 'Amen' may be true"? When you say "Amen" at Eucharist, do you think of yourself as a member of something larger than your own individual reception of the Lord?*

JOHN CALVIN

The Protestant Reformation in the sixteenth century began as protests against what certain clergy felt were excesses by the Roman Catholic Church. One of its preeminent leaders was John Calvin (1509–1564), who wrote about the body of Christ in his commentary on Romans 12:

> We are called on condition that we unite together in one body, since Christ has established among all who believe in Him the association and organic union which exists between members of the human body. And since men could not come into such a unity by themselves, He Himself became the bond of that union . . . . As the members of the one body have distinct powers, and all the members are distinct, since no member possesses all powers at the same time or assumes the offices of others, so also God has dispensed various gifts to us . . . . He has determined the order which He has desired us to maintain, so that each should regulate himself . . . and not thrust himself into the duties that belong to others. No one should seek to have all things at one time, but should be content with his lot, and willingly refrain from usurping the offices of others.

> . . . To prevent anyone from being grieved that he has
> not been given everything, [Paul] reminds us that each
> individual has his own responsibility assigned to him by
> the good purpose of God, because it is expedient for the
> common salvation of the body that no individual should
> be so furnished with the fullness of gifts as to despise
> his brethren . . . . . Each individual ought to be so intent
> upon bestowing his own gifts for the edification of the
> Church, that no one may relinquish his own functions
> and trespass on that of another. The safety of the Church
> is preserved by this most excellent order and symmetry,
> when every individual of himself imparts to the common
> good what he has received from the Lord without pre-
> venting others from doing so. To invert this order is to
> fight with God, by whose ordination it was appointed.[22]

Furthermore, like Paul, Calvin believed that any individual's
gifts belonged to the entire body, so that no one may deny or hide
his or her gifts or use them to his or her own advantage, as if they
were some sort of private treasury. In like manner, no one may
use his or her gifts over and against others. Misuse of gifts will
not occur if love is the defining attribute of the members, and if
members embrace the reality of community. Calvin expected the
body of Christ to function

> with the natural harmony of the human body. The body
> of Christ, accordingly, will be distinguished by such an
> inclination to mutual ministry as will enable us to for-
> sake all desires for "separate growth" and to do every-
> thing "for the common good." So much will our thoughts
> and energies be concerned with the other members of
> the body, and with the body as a whole, that "neither the
> benefits conferred" upon others, nor "our own particular
> sorrows" will prove distracting. On the contrary, they
> should direct our attention even more forcibly to the
> body.[23]

22. Calvin, *Epistles of Paul the Apostle*, 267–68.

23. Milner, *Calvin's Doctrine*, 186.

Making this point more forcibly in his *Commentary on Romans,* Calvin said,

> . . . the same wisdom which is observed in the human body ought to exist in the society of the faithful . . . . so God has dispensed to us various endowments, and, by this distinction, established among us an order he wished to be preserved; that each believer might regulate himself according to the measure of his own ability and not thrust himself into duties belonging to others; and that no individual might desire at the same time to have all, but, content with his own lot, voluntarily refrain from usurping the offices assigned to others. By expressly pointing out the communion that exists among us, he [i.e., God] clearly intimates how great diligence ought to be exerted for appropriating to the common good of the whole body of the church the powers which each member individually possesses . . . . Every person is desirous to have so great a supply as to stand in no need from his brethren; but the very bond of this mutual communication consists in no individual having sufficient for himself, but in his being compelled to borrow from others. I confess, therefore, that the society of the pious consists in each being contented with his own measure while he bestows upon his brethren the gifts, which he has received, and suffers himself to be assisted in turn by the gifts of others. But the apostle was particularly desirous to repress the pride, which he knew to be innate in mankind, and to prevent believers from being disappointed because all gifts were not bestowed upon them . . . . the good things of our heavenly Father are so distributed that each has a limited portion.[24]

Reflection Questions

1. *Which of Calvin's concepts particularly appeals to you? Why?*

2. *What surprised you about Calvin's words?*

24. Calvin, *Commentary on Romans,* 302–303.

3. *What do you make of his words, "But the apostle [Paul] was particularly desirous to repress the pride, which he knew to be innate in mankind, and to prevent believers from being disappointed because all gifts were not bestowed upon them . . . the good things of our heavenly Father are so distributed that each has a limited portion"? Have you witnessed believers being disappointed that they hadn't received certain gifts?*

SECOND VATICAN COUNCIL (1962–1965)

In the ensuing centuries after the Reformation, Protestants and Catholics tragically tended to regard each other suspiciously, each maintaining that they were right while the other was wrong. As a result, very little work was done on the doctrine of the body of Christ by either side. This rather tense state of affairs continued for nearly twenty years until the Second Vatican Council (1962–1965). In its document *Lumen Gentium*, the council fathers noted that

> All the members of the human body, though they are many, form one body, so also are the faithful in Christ (1 Cor 12:12). Also, in the building up of Christ's body, there is engaged a diversity of members and functions. There is only one Spirit who, according to His own richness and the needs of the ministries, gives His different gifts for the welfare of the Church (1 Cor 12: 1–11) . . . . Giving the body unity through Himself, both by His own power and by the interior union of the members, this same Spirit produces and stimulates love among the faithful. From this it follows that if one member suffers anything, all the members suffer with him, and if one member is honored, all the members together rejoice (1 Cor 12: 26).[25]

In its document on ecumenism *Unitatis Redintegratio*, the council recognized that "it remains true that all who have been justified by faith in Baptism are incorporated into Christ . . . . Moreover, some and even very many of the significant elements

25. Flannery, ed., *Vatican II, Lumen Gentium*, #7, 355.

and endowments which together go to build up and give life to the Church itself, can exist outside the visible boundaries of the Catholic Church."[26](par 3). In other words, the body of Christ encompasses all who belong to Christ.

PIUS PARSCH

Pius Parsch, a noted Catholic liturgist in the early twentieth century, wrote *We Are Christ's Body* (one of the few modern books exclusively about the body of Christ as community), summarizing the prevailing ideas about the topic of the time. His main points about the body as community and its comparison to the human body follow:

Headship of Christ:

> [The head] leads and controls the body . . . . If you want to walk, it is not sufficient that your feet have the power to move; they will not do so unless the head, so to speak, gives orders to this effect . . . . The head rules the entire body; every impulse, every movement, every perception . . . .[27]

> The body cannot live without the head; the head governs and activates the body—it thinks, it sees, it hears, it tastes, it feels . . . . Christ [the Head] is so intimately united with us that he is never apart from us for a moment.[28]

> A human body is . . . wonderful, not only in its unity but also in [its] diversity . . . . The most wonderful thing . . . about a human body is that it is alive . . . . From whence comes this life? From the soul. Only because it has a soul can the body feel and move and grow . . . . Head, body, and members all belong together; each can say to the others, "you belong to me, and I belong to you." . . . The

26. Flannery, ed., *Vatican II, Unitatis Redintegratio,* #3, 455.

27. Parsch, *We Are Christ's Body,* 17–18.

28. Parsch, *We Are Christ's Body,* 21.

head, body, and members are so intimately united that in all of them, there is but one life. No member can live by itself separately from the body.[29]

[In the Church] members have a common purpose and yet have individual lives . . . . [but there is also] the close union of its members and the sharing of life among them all.[30]

Need for members of the body to remain incorporated with it:

Whence does the body derive its life? . . . from the head. And whence does the Church derive her grace-life? From her head—Christ . . . . grace-life . . . . is Christ's life, divine life.[31]

Suppose a man's arms were so tightly bound with a ligature that the blood could no longer circulate in it, that arm would atrophy—it would die. Indeed, it would still be a member of the man's body—but a dead member. If the arm were amputated, then it would be quite impossible ever to restore it to life—it would be permanently dead. A Christian in mortal sin is like an atrophied or ligatured member of Christ's body; there is no grace-life in him. Yet it is still possible for this life to be restored because he is still a member of Christ's body.[32]

[Limbs and organs] have a permanent union with the body . . . . But if any one of them is amputated, it does not belong to the body any more . . . . members share one and the same life with the head and body . . . . they have not the same functions . . . . no member can be regarded as superfluous; each is needed in its own way, and each contributes in its own way to the welfare of the whole.[33]

29. Parsch, *We Are Christ's Body*, 26–27.

30. Parsch, *We Are Christ's Body*, 28.

31. Parsch, *We Are Christ's Body*, 32.

32. Parsch, *We Are Christ's Body*, 33.

33. Parsch, *We Are Christ's Body*, 38.

[Christians] . . . have a permanent union with the Mystical Body . . . for the rest of their lives, even though they be diseased or paralyzed members . . . . The members share one and the same life with the body and the head . . . members . . . live with Christ's life . . . . The members are not identical, but have differing functions and a due subordination to each other.[34]

. . . in the Mystical Body of Christ, we find the perfect example of community; it is based on the law of fraternal charity, and nothing harms it so much as disordered self-love.[35]

. . . all healthy members of the Mystical Body have a responsibility towards the sick members.[36]

. . . even if a Christian does sin grievously . . . he is still a member of Christ's Body—a sick or injured member for whose sake others must bestir themselves that the life-stream may flow to him again and make him sound.[37]

Importance of the diversity of function or roles:

The purpose of the hand . . . is to take hold of things; of the foot is to walk, or the ear to hear, of the eye to see, of the mouth to eat and to speak . . . . The purpose of each member is the most important and essential feature of it.[38]

. . . from all eternity, God has foreseen some particular . . . way of life for each person, involving some special task entrusted to him.[39]

34. Parsch, *We Are Christ's Body*, 38–39.

35. Parsch, *We Are Christ's Body*, 40.

36. Parsch, *We Are Christ's Body*, 43.

37. Parsch, *We Are Christ's Body*, 51.

38. Parsch, *We Are Christ's Body*, 67.

39. Parsch, *We Are Christ's Body*, 73.

Membership of the body extends beyond those who are currently alive:

> The phrase "I believe in the communion of saints" is a profession, therefore, of belief in the Mystical Body of Christ, in which all members are bound together by the closest ties . . . . There exists in the Mystical Body an ideal and most perfect sharing according to three principles: (i) each member has access to the common spiritual treasure of the whole body; (ii) the members help each other; whatever each one merits is of profit to all, and whatever each one possesses, he shares with all; (iii) the more gifted and exalted members have the duty of coming to the rescue of those who are weak and poor.[40]

> [This] mutual help . . . extends beyond earth throughout the communion of saints . . . .[41]

> We should do more than just pray for our fellow members of the Mystical Body—we ought also to . . . make reparation for others . . . . Just as Christ, in his earthly life, had to suffer in order to redeem us, so also . . . Christ's Mystical Body must endure a certain measure of suffering. And because of the unity among the members, all benefit from the sufferings of each one.[42]

Perhaps, we can summarize the tradition of the body of Christ as community with the words of historian Emile Mersch.

> It is Unity that sanctifies us and saves us; Unity alone can truly pray; Unity alone can be pleasing to God. For Unity is the body of Christ; it is Christ . . . . Ultimately, in the whole Church, there is only Christ, the Christ the Head and members. The hierarchy is nothing and the unity of the Church is nothing, apart from the Lord who continues to unite His own in Himself.[43]

40. Parsch, *We Are Christ's Body*, 87–88.

41. Parsch, *We Are Christ's Body*, 89–90.

42. Parsch, *We Are Christ's Body*, 93.

43. Mersch, *Whole Christ*, 395–96.

Reflection Questions

1. *How can the words of Chrysostom or Augustine be apropos today in our world?*

2. *How can entering into the mystery of the body of Christ begin to heal our world, our nation, our neighborhoods, our churches, and our families? How can doing so begin the process of our own healing?*

3. *Which aspect of the body of Christ will be the most difficult for your friends and family members to accept? Which aspect will be the most difficult for you to accept?*

Chapter 4

A Corpus Christi (Body of Christ) Spirituality

EVERY CELL IN THE HUMAN body has the same DNA as every other cell. It is in this way that each of the body's cells is marked as being part of the larger body and being part of other cells. In other words, they hold a common membership in a particular human body.

We have seen the attributes of the body of Christ from Paul's perspective: unity, diversity of gifts, interconnectedness, and concern for the least. These are the attributes of the body that distinguishes it from other bodies of individuals, such as political or social ones. These are the attributes that each member of the body must carry within him- or herself.

It is, perhaps, easier to understand how a body of believers, as a whole, would need to manifest these gifts than it is to see how an individual believer would need to do the same. Yet, just as the human body is composed of individual cells, the body of Christ is composed of individual members. Just as the cells in the body are connected by a common genetic identity, the members of the body of Christ are connected by a common spiritual identity: we belong to Christ, who marks us as his own.

Using Paul's four attributes of the corporate body of Christ, and realizing that each of us bears those attributes if we are truly members of that body, what would "Corpus Christi" spirituality look like for an individual believer?

UNITY

Because of hurts incurred early in life, many persons insist that they prefer to be alone and be their own master; they believe they do best as solo agents, because, in their view, other people get in their way.

Corpus Christi spirituality argues against that. Whether we like it or not, whether we believe it or not, we are in unity with other people. This is a divine design, not a human one. Furthermore, we are in unity with people who seem very unlike us and with people whom we might not even like. Personal feelings are irrelevant in terms of the reality of the unity. Personal feelings, however, play a large role in how we live out that unity in our individual lives.

A person who embraces Corpus Christi spirituality will see unity as a good and not as an impediment to personal success, because true success depends on the success of the whole. When one person or one group achieves some goal, those who embrace Corpus Christi spirituality see that achievement as their own because they are in union with those accomplishing the goal. For example, when apartheid collapsed in South Africa, those with Corpus Christi spirituality saw it as a success for the entire body of Christ and each member, regardless of where they lived. When people who were heretofore treated with contempt are now treated with dignity, it increases the dignity of each member of the body and the dignity of the body as a whole.

The person with Corpus Christi spirituality rejoices in unity and knows that noble human endeavors lift all who are united. Conversely, despicable human actions drag down all who are united, just as in the human body, when a serious illness affects every part of the body—*in some way*—and not just those parts that are most directly affected or those contiguous to the directly impacted part. Violence in a "dangerous" city affects the "safe" suburbs. Genocide in a distant part of the world truly affects the entire body and its members, regardless of whether the members have any connection with that part of the world.

DIVERSITY OF GIFTS AND ROLES

The person with Corpus Christi spirituality celebrates the fact that there is great diversity in the world, especially the diversity of human beings with their varied gifts and roles. Such diversity is liberating and not threatening.

And threatening it can be to those who believe in "safety in numbers" and who want to be surrounded by those who look or act like they do. Diversity can also be threatening to those who are dissatisfied with their own gifts or roles in life and to those who resent attention paid to persons who have gifts or roles which they do not possess.

Corpus Christi spirituality recognizes that God created and permits diversity for purposes not always immediately obvious. As a good son or daughter of that God, an individual with Corpus Christi spirituality knows that honoring, and even celebrating, diversity is honoring and celebrating the One who designed it in the first place.

As the early church fathers noted, envy of others' gifts is a natural human reaction to deprivation, but it is not to be an attribute of a member of the body of Christ. And, although it does seem farcical to imagine a tooth envying an eye in the human body, it is, perhaps, equally as farcical for a person who can't carry a tune to envy the cantor at mass. The human body needs eye and tooth; the church body needs both those who can sing and those who cannot. Most importantly, a body needs all its members.

Because we cannot always see the reason for our own gift or role, we tend to think as our cultural norms would have us think, and consider that certain persons *are* more important because there are more visible or have seemingly higher-status roles than we do. But the beauty of creation lies precisely in diversity of form and function, and that is true of the body of Christ, as well. Paul was right when he noted that "now we see through a mirror dimly, but then we shall see face to face" (1 Cor 13: 12). Our vision is dim now, but one day when we will be able to see clearly, it will all make sense; the pieces will all fall into place. That requires humility and patience in the present.

INTERRELATEDNESS

In our own society, we pride ourselves on being able to do things on our own without any help from others. Consider the jokes made about men failing to ask for directions when driving around lost or the jokes made about those who fail to read the directions that come with a new product. Our culture encourages us to see it as a sign of personal weakness if we need someone else's assistance—whether in person or in print—to get something done.

Corpus Christi spirituality knows that such a belief is foolishness. First of all, no one person can know everything. Secondly, a person who requires help is not necessarily weak. Thirdly, such a belief was not Christ's when he walked the earth, for he asked for what he needed—from fellow Jew and non-Jew alike.

When he lived as a human being, Christ accepted help from many people, who fed him, washed his feet, welcomed him into their homes, and enlarged his ministry. Christ did not seem to have the difficulty that many of his followers had (and still have) in asking for help. He did it openly. Furthermore, after the resurrection, he charged his followers to continue his work on earth. One imagines that with a "fiat," Christ could have done in a flash what has taken his followers centuries to do, but he resisted that temptation. He wants the members of his body to be his hands, feet, and voice in the world until he again returns.

Why do *we* persist in believing that we must do everything on our own in order to be mature? It is probably a residue from our childhoods when adults repeatedly told us to grow up or showed irritation when they needed to do something for us. Many of us resolved never to be in that situation again. The same is true for those whom life has treated unkindly, especially if the unkindness was perpetrated by a person on whom we depended. "I'll never get myself into *that* situation again," we vow. And although the reason for such a stance might be easily understandable, it doesn't translate to all situations in life, especially not our roles in the body of Christ.

The body of Christ was *designed* to elicit interrelatedness among all members, for no one member (except Christ himself) has all the gifts necessary to make the body flourish. And even Christ chooses to work with the members so that the joys can belong to all. A person with Corpus Christi spirituality understands his or her limitations and rejoices that there are others who can "fill in the gaps," all the while filling in the gaps for others who have different limitations.

To be sure, Corpus Christi spirituality requires thinking in terms of "we" rather than "I," and that is hard in our culture which so emphasizes "I." For individuals who need to promote *themselves* as unique, this "we" business seems bizarre. Yet, Corpus Christi spirituality doesn't see it as bizarre, but as reality. We affect others, and others affect us—each and every day, in trivial and not-so-trivial ways. For example, if I don't have enough money to pay for my groceries at the checkout counter and have to ask the checker to take some items off my tab, my failure to plan ahead will slow down the line, affecting everyone behind me. As a more serious example, if I choose to drink and drive, and, in doing so, cause a one-car accident on the expressway, cars will be backed up for miles if my vehicle is blocking the road.

Furthermore, Corpus Christi spirituality refuses to adopt a "them vs. us" mentality, no matter what the situation. In some profound way, "we" are frequently "them," and "they" are frequently "us." For example, we hear about persons with explosive tempers on the road, congratulating ourselves that we are not "them." Yet, at home, we yell and scream at our children, beyond all reason. In some way, "we" are the "them" whom we despised because of their angry behavior on the road.

In the body of Christ, there is *absolutely nothing to be gained* with an "us vs. them" mentality. We are all interrelated, and many can come to Christ through us and our own actions. Furthermore, others can contribute to our own re-conversion and maturation as members of the body.

PREFERENTIAL OPTION FOR THOSE WHO ARE THE LEAST

Corpus Christi spirituality understands that many of the "least" in the world did not become so because of anything that they themselves did. Their situation might be the result of global inequities, societal prejudices, or bad choices made by someone else. A person with Corpus Christi spirituality accepts that and looks out for those so affected.

But even those who are the "least" because of bad decisions they themselves have made (e.g., a person incarcerated for a crime he freely committed) are the focus of the care and concern of a person with Corpus Christi spirituality. One can detest the sin and love the sinner, precisely because the sinner is a child of God, made in God's image and likeness. In this, the person with Corpus Christi spirituality models him- or herself after Christ.

Christ welcomed those who came to him, healing people whom society had labeled as "outcasts" or "sinners." Furthermore, he ate with sinners, a constant accusation made by his enemies throughout his ministry. He engaged in conversation those whom the religious leaders of his time had deemed "nobodies," such as women and foreigners. He consistently praised the faith of those— regardless of their status or belief system—who had come to him for aid. Those with Corpus Christi spirituality emulate their Lord, knowing full well that the "least" are part of the body as much as they are. In fact, a reversal of roles sometimes occurs in which the "best" become the "least."

I think of an example in my own life. A few years ago, I was volunteering at a clinic for people lacking health insurance. One day, a young man, his wife, and their new baby came in. They were well-dressed and delightful, prompting me to wonder why they were at this clinic, whose clientele, for the most part, presented very differently. As I was examining the baby, the young man's eyes suddenly filled with tears, and his wife began to openly cry. When I asked what was wrong, he said, "This is a time when we should be so happy with our baby. But we're not. When my wife became pregnant, we both decided that she should quit her job in late pregnancy to take care of our baby, and I would support the family. So, she quit her job two months ago. Three weeks before the baby was born, my firm downsized, and I was terminated. I'm a mess. After all, I have an MBA. I've tried to do everything right; this shouldn't be happening to me."

Unfortunately, no one is immune to becoming the least in our society. A car accident, a natural disaster, a downsizing, a terminal illness—all of these can lead to our moving from "best" to "least," sometimes in the course of a single day. Furthermore, even those who have been the "best" for most of their lives can become the "least" as they age and experience age-related discrimination. A person with Corpus Christi spirituality knows all of this and always behaves in such a way as to give honor to all persons.

In our present culture, a person with Corpus Christi spirituality seems hopelessly out of it. Unity, interrelatedness, appreciation of diversity, and concern for the "least" are not the hallmarks of our time, and anyone who openly embraces such a mind-set will likely be labeled crazy, naïve, or suspect: crazy or naïve because such a person really believes that the world can be engaged in this way, or suspect because such a belief might undermine the actual way we live our lives. For example, most of us like some diversity in our lives . . . but not too much. We're warned to be wary of things too foreign to our culture. As another example, most of us like to think that we—as individuals or as a nation—are independent and need others only when we choose to do so. A constant state of interrelatedness does not fit into the cultural equation. Yet, interrelatedness is reality.

Because it is so difficult living counterculturally, a person with Corpus Christi spirituality must remain in close communication with Christ through praying (individual and communal), reading Scripture, and receiving Eucharist as often as he or she can. Corpus Christi spirituality models the spirituality of Christ, the head of the body. What better way to embrace the spiritual beliefs and practices of Christ than to remain closely connected with him in all things? And how best to be supported in this spirituality than by praying, reading Scripture, and receiving Eucharist, and serving others with those who embrace the same spiritual beliefs?

Reflection Questions

1. *In which ways would outsiders know you as a member of the body of Christ?*

2. *Which of the four attributes of Corpus Christi spirituality are most appealing to you, and why?*

3. *Which of the attributes are least appealing, and why?*

4. *In which ways do you have the need of growth?*

Chapter 5

The Growth of the Body of Christ

THE HUMAN BODY GROWS and develops in magnificent ways. For example, in the space of twelve short months, the tiny, helpless infant becomes a person who can move independently and say a few words. Or, as another example, in five short years, the giggly eight-year-old becomes a teenager, and in another few years after that, that teen becomes a young woman on her own. Not only does the human body grow larger but it develops cognitively, emotionally, socially, morally, and spiritually, capable of ever greater sophistication of thought and action.

Yet, no human body can grow or develop normally without the proper conditions for its growth, such as proper nutrition, rest, and physical activity. To grow optimally—to reach its full potential—the body needs to be protected from external and internal threats to its integrity, such as contagious agents and toxins, wounds, malignancies, and other physical and psychological conditions.

The body of Christ is like the human body in this way. The body is meant to grow ever larger and stronger, in member number and in its positive effect upon the world. To do that, every member in the body needs to seek such growth and development as a common goal. As each member grows and develops in Christ, the body as a whole grows and develops maturity in Christ.

In his book *Christly Gestures*, pastor Brett Webb-Mitchell's main thesis is that education is an important way of building up the body of Christ, not only in terms of new members but also in terms of established members. Learning is a lifelong project, no matter what the subject. And this learning is especially important in the body of Christ. After all, how do any of us really *know* what it means to be members of the body of Christ? Someone must show us what it means, must model the behavior for us. And, in the body of Christ, we learn together, for we are taught by many. That, in fact, is one of the main lessons to learn: that we are in community; what we learn (or fail to learn) affects others, and vice versa. What we do makes a difference in the lives of others, just as what they do makes a difference in our lives. How true this is in today's world, as the ways of the world sometimes become the ways of a faith community. Furthermore, if we are members of Christ's body, then Christ's "presence" (or lack thereof) in our world depends on the actions (or inactions) of us, the members.

In *Christly Gestures*, Webb-Mitchell wrote: "Instead of . . . the church as a collective of independent or interdependent individuals who live in a false individualism amid the world's temptations to be utterly selfish . . . [the body of Christ] is an individual organism in which each part is dependent not only on other members but also on the head of the body, Jesus Christ."[1] In other words, in the body of Christ, there is a group of individuals who have become something more than a mere collection of individuals, and, as such, they can contribute more as the body than they can as any single individual.

Living in such interdependence is not only countercultural but also jarring—to the one living in such a way and to those with whom he or she comes into contact. It is jarring precisely because we realize that we do not belong entirely to ourselves, and what we do does not affect only ourselves and our immediate circle of relatives, friends, and acquaintances. Webb-Mitchell noted:

1. Webb-Mitchell, *Christly Gestures*, 50.

The process of patterning into Christ will be awkward, difficult, and perhaps divisive at times, for in becoming members of Christ's body, we are required to take on ourselves a practice by which we learn that our bodies and lives are not our own but Christ's. Such patterning demands a lifetime of practice, not by ourselves but among members of the church, with its many disciplines, gifts, and services . . .[2]

Christians are called to willingly submit to the will of Christ's mind, body, and spirit . . . . One of the implications of this . . . radical submissiveness is that if my mind, body, and spirit are not mine alone, they are now the shared responsibility of the larger body of believers, of whom I am a part and to whom I am related and accountable.[3]

What, according to Brett-Mitchell, are these Christly gestures, gestures that if performed "well and often enough, they will become habitual"[4] and define us?

> . . . both offering money in a gesture of compassion and also extending friendship and hospitality . . . looking them in the eye, and sharing the peace of Christ with them.[5]

> Taking care of children who are sick because of a contaminated environment, being with those cast as outsiders in society and the church, standing in solidarity with those disabled and those without families, equipping those who are poor, preaching the Good News to those who thirst and hunger for it, showing hospitality to all who are strangers to us—these things are what it means to be doers . . . of the Word-become-flesh.[6]

2. Webb-Mitchell, *Christly Gestures*, 171.
3. Webb-Mitchell, *Christly Gestures*, 172.
4. Webb-Mitchell, *Christly Gestures*, 225.
5. Webb-Mitchell, *Christly Gestures*, 247.
6. Webb-Mitchell, *Christly Gestures*, 242.

> [Practicing] the gestures of *being with* those who are poor or distressed, listening to their needs rather than telling them what they *should* need; and together building what they need and want as they acquire a new sense of self-confidence in discovering the gifts and services that they—and we—can bring to Christ's body . . . .[7]

Indeed, these are the gestures described by centuries of church leaders. If we could behave in such ways, the body of Christ would grow in members and in its capacity to impact the world in very real ways, because the goodness of its members and their actions would be beacons of light in a deeply darkened world. The impact would attract new members and result in growth. As Webb-Mitchell noted, "Growth [of the body] comes through the practice of compassion, patience, forgiveness, and love—all of those activities of the mind and spirit nourishing the body, but also activities in which the body is held fast to the head and to the heart."[8]

These gestures are the "lifestyle" of the body of Christ. Each day, we hear how lifestyle choices affect the human body—for good or for ill. This is as true for infants and children as it is for adults. Without proper nutrition, infants and small children are often hampered in their growth. Without proper nutrition, adults incur preventable illnesses. Without proper rest, children and teens do not learn as well. Without proper rest, adults cannot think clearly. Without proper exercise, children and teens become sedentary, setting them up for a future of preventable chronic conditions. Without proper exercise, adults become weaker than they should be.

Although we are called to imitate Christ, becoming more like Christ each day, membership in the body of Christ does not require that we become clones of Christ or any other member. Nor does it require that all members be homogenized, for we are each equipped to witness in a unique way. To use a cooking image, instead of melting all the ingredients (members) together in a slurry or porridge, each ingredient (member) is allowed to contribute its

7. Webb-Mitchell, *Christly Gestures*, 240.
8. Webb-Mitchell, *Christly Gestures*, 85.

own flavor, as in a stew, where the various ingredients can be easily seen for what they are. All the ingredients make up the unique flavor and texture of the stew, and without any one of the ingredients, the stew would lose a little something. Yet, none of the ingredients alone are the stew. Without each of us, the body of Christ is a little poorer, although none of us are the body of Christ without the others.

Webb-Mitchell summarized John Howard Yoder's thought from *Body Politics*: "the modern world hopes that divisions among human beings can be overcome by summing up our individual parts, leaving significant parts of our lives behind in order to become part of a bland-tasting 'melting pot.'"[9] Jesus came to set the world on fire (Luke 12:49), and Christian blandness will hardly result in even a smoldering. In the body of Christ, the mystery is that we retain our individuality (even as cells in the body retain their individual natures) while being part of something much larger, the balance of the individual and the community. A living laboratory for this educational experience is one's church community. "The function of a group like the church is to aid people in achieving together what they cannot possibly achieve alone."[10] "A mutual intercommunication of seemingly independent parts of the body produces an integrated harmony, richer than one unit or body part acting alone."[11]

In this way, our churches both grow in members and (more importantly) maturity. After all, the human body does not only grow in size; it becomes more developed, capable of more sophisticated actions. So, too, our congregations. Although many church communities define success as numerical growth, it is much more. It is maturation. Maturation of the community is predicated on maturation of individual members. Each of us can start small in our local churches, as we learn to be authentic members of the body of Christ. Such a living role prepares us well for our role in the larger body of Christ. This is done in spite of the fact that we

9. Webb-Mitchell, *Christly Gestures*, 53.

10. Webb-Mitchell, *Christly Gestures*, 60.

11. Webb-Mitchell, *Christly Gestures*, 74.

are all sinners, and we have to make adjustments for each other's sinfulness in this world—whether in our local churches or in the larger world. This means that we recognize that individualism is not a synonym for authenticity. Throughout his book, Webb-Mitchell noted how important community is. Four important points follow:

1. Many of us who are part of the "baby boom" generation have also experienced the "me" decade. The radical "in-dividual," or "un-divided one," is a single . . . entity, isolated and claiming that he or she is unique, not part of a community of people . . . The real problem of radical individualism is selfishness and stridency, which are contrary to life in Christ's body . . . the focus [of which] is on the many who make up the one body . . . they are becoming more like Christ and thus less like themselves.[12]

2. In the body of Christ, we are constantly looking out for the needs of other people first rather than necessarily thinking of ourselves and our own self-centered needs. This means letting go of petty resentments . . . .[13]

3. [Reflecting on Jean Vanier's words] We are sinners, and yet we are created to live in relationship with other people—who are also sinners—in the body . . . . it is necessary for a community to have individuals who are difficult to live with: they make the community "interesting," and they also reveal the strengths and weaknesses in our churches . . . . conflict is often important in helping a community understand what it means to live as a community.[14]

4. [Again, reflecting on Vanier] The body of Christ must discern together; they must have a sense of how to share authority in a gathering, and they must supply the overwhelming support that is necessary

---

12. Webb-Mitchell, *Christly Gestures*, 80.

13. Webb-Mitchell, *Christly Gestures*, 81.

14. Webb-Mitchell, *Christly Gestures*, 82–83.

for each person to grow and be better able to carry responsibility for the up-building of the body.[15]

Undeniably, there are many temptations facing local churches and their leaders. To name but three:

1. The sin of "autonomy," *self-sufficiency*, or the "right to do what I like" (6:12) is precisely the "fleshly" attitude within the church (3:1–4), which Paul finds alien to Christlike existence "for others," but reflects much secular culture (whether inside or outside the church) at the beginning of the twenty-first century.[16]

2. Racial prejudice and social stereotypes [that] are supposed to be submerged and put to death in baptism, but all too frequently these evils survive the experience, dry themselves off, and form cankers on the body . . . Paul affirms that in Christ—and only in Christ—are these ethnic and sociological differences negated. What may polarize the world does not or should not divide the church.[17]

3. . . . when . . . differences [of opinion] are combined with a lack of acceptance of others, so that a section of the church hardens itself against the rest and behaves as if it were self-contained . . .[18]

Church leadership can also grow weary, failing to exercise their leadership in a manner that builds up the body of Christ. All of these can impact us from within and stunt member and church growth and development.

And not much has changed in the last eighty-five years. In 1938, historian Mersch noted: "Suffering, humiliation, and penance, all consequences of our faults remain in the Mystical Body of which we are members. But in this body, because of the Christ who is its Head, they become a healing remedy; far from impeding

15. Webb-Mitchell, *Christly Gestures*, 236.

16. Thiselton, *First Epistle to the Corinthians*, 1006.

17. Garland, *1 Corinthians*, 592.

18. Banks, *Paul's Idea of Community*, 68.

the full development of the organism and the free exercise of all its powers, they help both to extend and to strengthen it."[19]

As is the situation with the human body, sometimes the conditions in the world are not always conducive to optimal growth and development—not for individuals, not for local churches, and not for the body of Christ. To reiterate, growth in size does not necessarily translate into growth in authenticity. What types of threats get in the way of our becoming more Christlike and more transparent as members of his body?

THREATS TO GROWTH

In terms of threats to human bodies, it seems that every day, there are news stories about infectious agents that damage living creatures, especially human beings, and that some of these agents are resistant to the usual drugs that once would have treated the illnesses they cause. We need only recall E coli. contamination of food, methicillin-resistant staphylococcus aureus, and COVID to realize how frequent these news stories have become. We are also always reminded about the numerous toxins in our environment, toxins that can cause cancer, genetic defects, or death from other causes. Clearly, these threats can prevent the normal growth and development of anyone who comes into contact with them.

But there are other external threats that make normal growth and development unlikely. As an example, consider violence. Children who are treated violently or abusively are unlikely to develop normally, and, in the cases in which they incur physical trauma, they might not even grow normally. Since development is a lifelong process, even adults who are treated violently or abusively might not be able to develop as fully as their potential might permit. This is true of violence at the hands of a stranger as well as violence at the hands of someone known to the victim. It is true of a one-time violent episode as well as it is of repeated or chronic violent episodes.

19. Mersch, *Whole Christ*, 439.

Some of our cities are very violent places, and many people cannot grow and develop normally because of that violence. The violent culture is all around them; it pervades the air that they breathe. In addition, across the world, there are many war-torn lands, where it seems that no one is immune from the effects of violence. How can one learn to trust in such environments? How can one's growth and development flourish in the midst of violence, especially when it is not at all evident that one can even *survive* in the midst of that violence? Sadly, even some of our churches are violent in their own ways, as some members destroy other members through gossip. Galatians 5:15 is as true today as it was when first written: "But if you bite and devour one another, watch out that you are not consumed by one another."

So, too, there are many external threats that impact the body of Christ. Those who advocate the use of violence ridicule the Christian belief of "turn the other cheek" and those who believe in peacemaking. Societal attitudes such as prejudice and xenophobia assault various members of the body. A hedonistic lifestyle, marked by materialism and secularism, makes moral Christians seem quaint, if not downright foolish. These external threats can become internal threats to the well-being of the body of Christ if enough members of the body subscribe to them. It's as if members of the body turn against the body, or try to separate themselves from it.

Proper growth and development of the human body can only occur if the right nutrients are ingested, for how can the body make healthy body cells, organs, and systems with unhealthy or inferior materials? Yet, each day, we hear about the epidemic of obesity in this country and other Western countries which are wealthy enough to assure adequate and healthy foodstuffs for their people. Obesity usually results from ingesting too many sugary or fatty foods and not getting enough exercise. Our bodies can become out of shape, and we tire at the least exertion.

So, too, the body of Christ can be prevented from its full growth and development if it has an intake of "light" spiritual ideas and very little exercise in terms of active works of charity for others. Many persons prefer to read popular writers rather than Scripture, or New Age writers rather than venerated Christian writers. I will say more about this issue in a later chapter.

In addition, many individuals do not get enough exercise in their faith, as they live in their heads more than in their hands, and certainly more than in their hearts. These members of the body sit at home or in their churches and imagine themselves engaged in meaningful activities rather than actually doing so. They can think of many different strategies to live their faith but fail to do the work involved to actually get something done.

Our physical bodies need the proper rest; the same is true of the body of Christ. But, instead of thinking of rest as mere sleep, we are called to actively rest in the Lord. We are called to "waste time" with God, with no purpose other than to just be with the One who called us into existence and sustains us at every moment. Our physical bodies break down, become ill, and even perish without the proper rest. When we are fatigued, we drag ourselves through our days, unable to give our best. This continues until our bodies put a halt to our sleep deprivation and become ill, forcing us to finally rest. When we, as members of the body of Christ, fail to rest in the Lord, we drag ourselves through life, unable to give our best to Christ and to our fellow members. This often continues until some crisis reminds us to whom we belong, paving the way for us to return to resting in the Lord.

Finally, proper growth of the human body also requires healthy breathing and an appropriate intake of oxygen. Without oxygen, the human body dies. In fact, we know from those affected by drowning, stroke, or heart attack that if the brain is denied oxygen for seven minutes, irreparable brain damage can begin to occur. Oxygen is necessary for every single biological process in our bodies.

When we inhale, we take in oxygen from the air; when we exhale, we release carbon dioxide from our bodies, which is a waste product for us. Too much carbon dioxide is bad for human beings, while carbon dioxide is necessary for plants. In fact, plants release oxygen for our use, as we release carbon dioxide for their use—quite an exquisite example of interrelatedness. If we fail to inhale for a period of time, we die, and if we cannot exhale for a period of time, we die.

Inhalation is also called inspiration, literally "taking in of air or spirit." That means that if we fail to inspire, we die. That can be physically true, but it also can be spiritually true. If we, as members of the body of Christ, fail to breathe in the Spirit, if we fail to receive "inSpiration," we will not be able to persevere. The Spirit is as necessary to members in the body as oxygen is to cells in the human body. We are dead without the enlivening power of the Spirit.

And just as what we human beings release is used by plants for their life (and vice versa), the same is true in the body of Christ. We are called to inspire other members, and they are called to inspire us. We are there for Christ *and for each other,* just as the cells in the physical body are there for the body as a whole and for other individual cells. The example of some members of the body (e.g., Desmond Tutu, Mother Teresa) can inspire the other members to do greater things in their own lives. But one need not be famous to be a source of inspiration; many good people live faithfully each and every day without a lot of fuss, and in doing so, they build up the body of Christ. Members of the body are interdependent, and the good that one does affects us all, as does the evil that one does. Furthermore, since we are all related to each other, when there are needs, we are called to supply those needs for each other; others supply our needs, while we supply theirs. In such an existence, nothing is wasted, and no one need be in want of anything, for there truly is enough to go around to sustain life and even encourage its flourishing. This is how the body grows and develops in a vibrant way, and it can only happen when we all appreciate the fact of how interrelated we are.

St. Paul and the fathers of the church believed that the body of Christ had almost limitless growth potential. Do we honestly feel the same way today? They felt that every opportunity to add a member to the body should be exercised. Do we believe that today, and if so, what do we do about it?

The development of the human person is a lifelong process; so, too, with the body of Christ. The body's development is limited by its human members but has the potential of its divine head. The body can develop greater spiritual and moral maturity—in thought, word, and deed—mirroring the maturity of Christ. Do we believe that, and are we willing to make the sacrifices in our own lives to ensure that we play our own part in the development of the body? Do we ourselves want to grow and develop in our own lives so that we can make a positive contribution to the body of Christ?

Growth and development are always possible . . . until the day we die. Growth and development of the body of Christ are always possible and not limited by time and space, because of the limitless potential of our divine head, which, as the church fathers noted, he imputed to his members. But merely believing in the divine, limitless potential is not enough; we must also be willing to act upon that belief. We must be willing to grow and develop, even when it is uncomfortable. After all, *it's not about us.* It is about Christ and the reign of God upon the earth. The body of Christ can grow and develop *precisely* because of the great potential that is given to it by Christ himself.

Reflection Questions

1. *What marks a mature person—morally and spiritually?*

2. *In which of these areas do we need to mature?*

3. *How can we move toward maturity in the body of Christ?*

4. *How can we help others to do the same?*

5. *How does our congregation need to grow or mature?*

6. *What might be our role in such a process?*

Chapter 6

The Body of Christ
and Woundedness

How HARD IS IT for you to think of Christ wounded in the here and now? Because we think of the triumphant Christ, it is often hard for us to think of Christ as wounded *now*. Of course, we know that he was wounded on the cross, long ago, but after his resurrection, he is now immune from such pain.

But if we take seriously Matthew 25, "Whatever you do to the least of these, you do to me," we come to understand that Christ identifies so closely with his people that when they are hurt, he is hurt. This is true no matter where his people are; it is his global identity. Although it would be difficult to physically hurt Christ, it is possible to wound him by wounding those whom he loves. We can do this by actively hurting others (e.g., discrimination) or passively hurting them (e.g., ignoring or forgetting them). In some ways, being forgotten is worse than being actively hurt, since when one is forgotten, it's as if one is not important enough to matter. At least when one is actively wounded, there is still some engagement—albeit negative—with another person.

Being wounded is part and parcel of being human. Sometimes, the wounds are little more than slights; at other times, they are huge lacerations of our psyche and spirit. As the church fathers have noted, Christ identifies so closely with us, that he experiences *all* of our sorrows with us, no matter how seemingly insignificant.

We can wound our bodies by failing to take proper care of them: by "forgetting" to take medications, to watch our diets, to exercise, and to get enough rest. We can wound our bodies by taking unreasonable risks (e.g., driving after drinking). We can also intentionally wound our bodies by self-injuries behaviors, such as "cutting," a practice popular among some troubled youth.

In all these cases, we fail to take the goodness of our bodies seriously. Perhaps, we hate a certain body part, or we hate our very physicality because it seems crude. Perhaps we would prefer to be spirits, unencumbered by a body at all.

So too, in the body of Christ. We "forget" to care for the body by taking care of its members, especially those who are society's outcasts. We wound the body by engaging in activities that are not life-giving but death-dealing, such as addictive behaviors. We wound the body by experimenting with beliefs and practices that are completely at odds with our Christian heritage, especially those of certain New Age sects. We intentionally wound the body when we knowingly say or do things that will hurt fellow members of the body, as when we disparage those whom we do not consider to be our equals.

Yet, although we can wound ourselves, wounds frequently come from the outside. And so it is with the body of Christ. How is the body—Christ the head and the members—wounded from the outside?

Christ is wounded by the assaults on him and his followers by the prevailing culture of the world. In a culture that believes that violence is a perfectly acceptable form of problem resolution, the Prince of Peace and his followers look weak and foolish. In a culture that lionizes those with the most money or prestige, anyone who espouses a preferential option for the poor seems insane or a "do-gooder." In a culture that applauds massive spending by individuals and by societies in general, a belief system that calls for less (not more) seems unrealistically Spartan.

These are not just subtle messages; they are overt. Christ himself is mocked and trivialized, just as he was when the Roman soldiers were scourging him prior to his execution. Artists display obscene images of Christ or the saints in an effort to catch a little notoriety for themselves. Novelists and filmmakers create story lines that stretch credibility and border on the blasphemous. Christ is "cut down to size" by those who wish to think of him only as a good man, someone who is no better than we are. Famous (and not-so-famous) people liberally use Christ's name sloppily or profanely in their language, although they fail to use other famous peoples' names in such a crude way. If the way that many of us talk and behave is any indication, Christ is not taken seriously, even by those who claim to be members of his body. It is almost as if Christ is a make-believe figure, good for Sunday morning sermons, but not for the nitty-gritty of life. We might not be able to change the prevailing culture so that he is not mocked, but we certainly can monitor our own behavior, our words and actions.

Christ can certainly take care of himself, but it is the wounds of his followers—who can't always take care of themselves—that causes the deepest lacerations in the body of Christ.

Many of those who belong to Christ are marginalized. The little children whom Christ so loves are despised and permitted to starve to death in many countries; to die of preventable diseases in many poorer lands; or to be killed on violent streets across the globe, even in our own land. In other lands, they are abused through forced labor, combat, or sexual activity. They are treated as *things* rather than beloved *children,* members of Christ's very body. In still other, more prosperous, lands, children are pampered beyond any limits and encouraged to really believe that they are, indeed, better than others. Although they might be encouraged to give to others, it is a hierarchal giving, rather than a mutual sharing of gifts. Many of these children do not know anyone who is old, sick, poor, or in any kind of need, so they can only imagine the messages that they have been told about others. They do not have the opportunity to learn how others can minister to them. In a self-sufficient society, they do not need anything from anyone else anyway.

But, of course, all of this holds true only when it is convenient to have children around. At other times, when they seem to be a nuisance, they are hidden away. The beloved children are treated as nuisances rather than as full members of the body of Christ. Those without children want to live in places where there are no children. Those who work with young children in child care centers or homes fail to make a realistic wage. This treatment of children even, sadly enough, extends to our churches. When children come to church, some congregants glare at them and their parents if the children make the least amount of noise; sadly, some of the clergy do the same. In many congregations, children are excluded from having any kind of meaningful role. Adolescents are mistrusted, or they are made the brunt of hostile, suspicious, or disparaging comments.

Many will protest: "We love children!" Of course, we usually love the children who belong personally to us, while ignoring or frankly despising the children of others, especially if they don't look or talk like our children. Yet, they all belong to the body of Christ.

Society often despises those who place a drain on the economy—the children of poor people whom we have to feed; their poor parents themselves, especially if they do not speak "our" language; the beggars on the streets; those addicted to drugs or alcohol; the mentally ill; the school dropouts; the imprisoned; the frail elderly who live in so-called "homes"; the ill who linger too long. Sometimes, we buy into society's view of others rather than recalling the words of Matthew 25.

Society frequently despises those who are different—the children and parents whose religious belief system is different from our own; the people in the world who disagree with our foreign or domestic policy; the people who have different political views than we have; the people whose skin color is darker (or lighter) than our own; the people who can't speak the language most people speak;

the people who are much older (or younger) than we are. Our "forgetfulness" of the words of Matthew 25 indicts us.

Psychologists have noted that when a person despises one of his or her physical features, the person's entire self-esteem can suffer. If others tell a person, for example, that she has a big nose, she will probably start believing it. She might come to hate her nose so much that she becomes convinced that it is an impediment to her success. With it, she will believe that she is just not as good as she could be with a different nose. If she has the means, she might try to alter her nose surgically; otherwise, she will have to live with it. But by listening to what others say (whether it is objectively true or not) and hating her nose, such a person only hurts herself since her nose is part of her; it has the same DNA as the rest of her. If it is doing its job, why focus on appearances, which can be deceiving?

So, too, in the body of Christ. If we buy into society's warped views of other beloved children of God, we begin to despise certain members of the body of Christ because they don't fit in with what we think they should be. They don't fit the image of a beloved child of God, a member of Christ's body, which turns out to look more and more like ourselves. Such myopia, in the end, not only hurts ourselves, but the entire body of Christ. Admittedly, some people—at least on the surface—do not seem to be pulling their weight in our highly competitive, economic society. Maybe they are, and maybe they're not. Looks can be deceiving, as the church fathers repeatedly noted.

Even if some people are not pulling their weight, they provide the other members of the body an opportunity to minister to them. Without them, we lack an opportunity to serve and, in turn, be served by them. If we are called to serve them in some way, the mutuality of the body parts means that they are called to serve us in some way. As in the human body, we are often unaware what various body parts do for us . . . especially if we don't like them. What has an arthritic, crooked thumb done for the rest of the body lately? Perhaps assist in washing the other hand so that it can be clean or hold a fork so that the whole body can get food! What has a large nose done for the rest of the body? Perhaps smell the odor of smoke that permits a family to escape a fire or smell the wonderful aroma of fresh flowers! If such annoying parts of the body were suddenly removed, what would happen to the rest of the body? In like manner, the question is not what a beggar can do for us, or what an inmate on death row can do for us. The question is what roles do these individuals play in the life of the body of Christ. How do they assist the body's growth, and how do they interact with us so that we, too, in that interaction, contribute to the body's growth?

In the body of Christ, it is not our place to decide who's in and who's out. That is up to God. Webb-Mitchell wrote, "Christ's body has members, whom God created, Christ calls, and the Spirit infuses and marks for eternity."[1] We are to accept who is present as our sister and brother, even if we are completely incapable of discerning his or her purpose in the body. It is simply *not about us.*

Looking beyond our own circle of acquaintances and even our own society, there are others in the body of Christ with whom we have little in common . . . or so it seems. They are off our radar screen; they are easy to forget. We certainly don't wish them ill, but we don't work for their betterment either. What are any of us really doing for starving people in countries far from our homes, whether in our own country or in countries far from our country? Perhaps we think that there are too many starving people worldwide for us to be concerned about. Perhaps we are troubled by such needs but cannot possibly see how we, on our own, can make a difference.

In our body, even the little toe that is, relatively speaking, the farthest body part from the head, is taken care of by the wisdom of the body. If the toe is injured, inflammatory cells rush to it to start the healing process. This is true whether we hate the appearance of that toe or not; the body takes care of its own. And, if we should break our little toe, we will find out just how important it is. We will not be able to walk normally until it is healed. While it is injured and we walk in such a way to protect it, we might throw other body parts out of line, causing even more discomfort to the

1. Webb-Mitchell, *Christly Gestures,* 84.

entire body than just the pain of a broken toe. These effects are true whether we love our toe or hate it; whether it was wounded by our miscues (e.g., walking into a chair) or by the actions of others (e.g., having someone drop a large object on the foot). Pain is pain, no matter how it happens. A wound is a wound, no matter who or what caused it. The goodness of a well-functioning human body is that it takes care of its own, no matter how insignificant the part might seem or how unattractive it might be. It belongs to the entire body, and when it is hurt, the entire body is not quite right until the ailing part is on the road to healing and health. Depending on the body part wounded, the entire body might have to readjust itself to compensate for the loss of function of that injured body part.

And when our entire body is out of alignment, our psyche may also move to a more ominous place. After all, most of us fixate on an ailing body part. Perhaps it interferes with our movement, sleep, or appetite. When the injured part doesn't improve quickly, we might be cranky and frustrated, even wishing that we could remove the offending body part that is giving us so much trouble. Because we are concerned about the trouble in the present, it is difficult for us to take the long view of the worth of this part—in the past and in the future.

So, too, in the body of Christ. When we fixate anxiously or even angrily (e.g., "why don't *they* keep quiet or just get over it?") on those body members who are wounded, we forget the wisdom of the body and to whom we belong. When hurting members don't seem grateful for our help (or openly spurn it), we want to "cut them off." We get cranky and frustrated, seeking methods to either "fix" the offending people or to put them completely out of our minds so that they will not trouble our sleep and equanimity any longer. How foolish that is! Would we cut off our toe because it is broken? Would we cut off our ear because we don't hear as well as we used to hear? Would we cut out our heart because we had a heart attack?

So, what can we do? First, we can focus on Christ's imperatives and not on society's views. That is admittedly difficult, since society's views are like the air—all around us; we literally inhale them. Nevertheless, we need to focus on Christ—by praying, by reading Scripture, by worship. Frequent reception of Eucharist will strengthen our bond with him.

Second, we need to get our facts straight about those who are not like us. Simply accepting prevailing cultural views is like glibly accepting someone's opinion about our looks; the person might be right, but he might be wrong. We can learn in any way that seems most appropriate to us, but usually, the best learning comes experientially. That means actually working with the poor, the marginalized, those who are not like us. It means getting out of our comfort zones. Like examining a much-maligned body part more closely, we might find these individuals have a beauty all their own.

Third, we need to come clean with our own biases and prejudices. Human beings can sometimes wound themselves—either intentionally or unintentionally. When we despise fellow members of the body of Christ, we wound ourselves and the integrity of that body. How do *we* do this? What thoughts, words, or actions betray *our* true feelings about others? How can the world know *we're* serious about following Christ if we continuously try to amputate a part of the body? How can *we* be persons of integrity without repentance and a renewed commitment to be in solidarity with all those with whom we share membership in the body?

Reflection Questions

1. *In what ways have you been wounded in the past? How were you treated by those who knew of your hurt?*

2. *Who are the most wounded persons in your congregation? In general, how are they treated?*

3. *Has your congregation lost members who believed that they had been hurt by fellow congregants? What was done to try to retain them?*

4. *Which members of the body of Christ do you (or your congregation) tend to forget? Why?*

Chapter 7

The Body of Christ and Pathogens or Toxins

As we saw in the last chapter, the body of Christ can be wounded by societal practices that become our own. Like the human body, the body of Christ can be assailed by outside threats that wound the entire body.

TOXINS

When these outside threats to the human body are nonliving but harmful, we call them toxins. Toxins can't be spread from one person to another, but they can wreak great harm on the various organs of the body. Toxins can include such natural heavy metals as mercury and lead, and also human-made compounds. Some toxins are quickly fatal in any dose, while others are fatal if not promptly treated. Other toxins cause illness that is not necessarily fatal.

What kinds of toxins can affect the body of Christ? One example is an attitude of materialism and consumerism. In such an attitude, *things* are more important than people. With this mind-set, it is not so much what we are as what we have; the more we have, the better we are. It is not so much what we save as what we use; the more we use, the better we are. In this mind-set, more is always better, and less is seen as deprivation. Not only are material goods more important than people, but these material goods must be frequently replaced and flaunted, because there is always something new (which we need to have). Furthermore, what good is having something if others do not realize that we have it? The media preach this message more ubiquitously and consistently than homilists preach about God in a church: more is better and new is best. In such an attitude, there is little respect for the old (unless it will result in more material goods or money). Tradition takes a poor second place to novelty.

The media give the strong message that one isn't successful unless one is using (or wearing) the newest brand or driving the latest car. Failure to comply with this message means that one is hopelessly out of it. And, so, there is a never-ending quest for more and more, not always because people want to be on such a treadmill, but because they're afraid to jump off. Because no one can keep up with the constant need to be seen with the latest and newest, it is a frustrating way of life. One can never be satisfied, because there will always be something new (or better) just around the corner. But instead of dissuading us from living in such an "up-hill" manner, we become addicted to a certain way of life, and even look down on others who do not espouse it. Such an attitude can pollute the way the live our lives, as we must constantly struggle to "have it all."

Inevitably, such a toxin can affect the body of Christ. When things become more important than people, the members of the body of Christ can be discounted, especially those who can never fulfill societal expectations. After all (in a thought first voiced by Chrysostom), is it more important to have fine decorations in our churches than it is to ensure that the poor who come to our churches have something to eat or a place to lay their heads at night? Is it more important for us to procure expensive altar cloths or vestments than it is to provide warm clothing in the winter and serviceable clothing in the summer for those who work in menial jobs? Is it more important to spend thousands of dollars on a wedding reception than it is to provide meals for homeless men who are mentally challenged? Is it more important to have an expensive headstone for a deceased person's grave than it is to provide health care for a living person?

As biblical scholars and church fathers have noted, many churches want to showcase their more affluent members in an attempt to attract additional affluent members. Rarely do they want to showcase those members who dress poorly or can't speak well, for how would those members attract "important" people to join the church? This speaks to the materialism of our culture, a sad commentary on the relative worth of things and money over living members of the body of Christ. We can almost hear Jesus speaking about the Pharisee and the publican, the former as the "respectable" member of the synagogue, and the latter as the "unacceptable" member.

The fixation on the material also reminds us of the parable of the rich fool who wanted to store up his surplus in barns (Luke 12:16–21); we learn that his accumulation of wealth could not help him, as he would die soon. In the parable, Christ said, "So will it be for the one who stores up treasure for himself but is not rich in what matters to God." It also reminds us of the story of the rich young man who wanted to follow Jesus but just couldn't part with his many possessions (Mark 10:17–27). Jesus' words ring true today: "It is easier for a camel to pass through the eye of a needle than for one who is rich to enter the kingdom of God" (v. 25).

When material goods become more important than members of the body, they have also become more important than Christ himself, since Christ identifies with those members, as Matthew 25 reveals. The toxins of materialism and consumerism have devastating effects on the way that some members of the body regard other members of the body and Christ himself. For example, some people prefer to buy and then adorn themselves with an expensive crucifix rather than donate the price of that crucifix to an outreach ministry.

When people protest, "But I worked hard for this money! I should be able to do with it what I wish," they are not being bad, but they are thinking as independent individuals and not as interdependent members of the body of Christ. There is nothing wrong with wanting to wear a crucifix, but there is nothing right about ignoring human need in order to do so. The interdependence that Paul prized so highly is not the highest good of those who prefer their own wants over others' needs. As members of the body, we are called to work for the greatest good, even—and especially—if it doesn't directly benefit us.

PATHOGENS

Toxins affect people directly but not necessarily through other people. A pathogen affects others through people.

With regard to the human body, when these outside threats are living organisms, we call them pathogens. Pathogens include viruses, bacteria, and parasites. They are contagious, meaning that other living entities can "catch" them. Pathogens can be spread from one person to another. Depending on the condition of the person, pathogens might cause a range of conditions from the trivial to the deadly. The COVID epidemic is a good example of this.

One pathogen that can affect the body of Christ is that of prejudice or bias. It is a pathogen because it is so easily passed to others. For example, a man has a negative experience with someone of a different race. He tells his friends about the episode, and they are sympathetic and maybe even a bit angry over the way he was treated. Some of them might also adopt this prejudice, especially if they themselves have had little experience with people of that race. And so, the pathogen spreads from one to another, as these individuals pass it on to their friends and family members by saying, "I know a man who was treated badly by one of those people. They are not nice; watch your back when you're around them." If the pathogen is large enough or strong enough, it can spread rapidly, potentially wreaking havoc on innocent people. This is especially true in small, insular communities. Just as a germ spreads rapidly in a closed area (e.g., a dormitory), biases and prejudices can also spread rapidly in a small community. In a small area, the threat seems very real, and people believe what they want to believe, especially in the absence of factual information.

Probably one of the most virulent pathogens that can affect the body of Christ is that of gossip. Most people are not above a bit of gossip. Although it is not good, it is not necessarily evil. The kind of gossip that is evil is that which seeks to destroy another person. Like a pathogen, it can spread throughout a church community, as one person tells another, and that person tells yet another, and so on. Soon, the entire community is whispering about something that might or might not be true. Gossip has the potential to be so virulent because it destroys the unity that should be intrinsic to the body of Christ. Gossip makes a mockery of that unity, as people, engaged in malicious gossip, are not thinking about the good of the whole but only about self-interests. In such a climate, unity is impossible.

During the COVID pandemic, we repeatedly heard the term "super-spreader events," events in which many people are close together in a limited space. The events themselves are not bad, but during a pandemic, the events facilitate the spread of germs. In terms of gossip, especially gossip that wounds or even leads to someone's death, social media is like a super-spreader event. In itself, it may not be evil, but given the right conditions, it can cause an explosion of true and false gossip to spread, ruining lives in the process.

Just as in the world of infectious disease, if a pathogen can occur in small communities, it certainly can (and does) occur on a larger scale. After all, it is easy for us to accept the societal practice of vilifying those who are the "other," imputing to them all sorts of evil thoughts, words, and actions, of which we, of course, would never be guilty. They are *not* like us, and since we are the measure of what a good person (or member of the body) should be, the conclusion is that they are not good. This conclusion seems especially true when we consider people who live in far-off lands or who have vastly different cultural practices than we do. "Why can't they be more like us?" we moan. Sometimes, in a misguided attempt to create people just like us, we attempt to force our ways upon them. Or we force them to act in certain ways that benefit us, treating them as means to an end rather than people in their own right. In the human body, this would be akin to a virus making the ear an organ of smell. Differences exist for a reason. This is as true in nature as in human beings as in the body of Christ.

Look at the great variety of trees, insects, birds, flowers; why must there be so many? Why can't they all be the same? Variety and differences are to be celebrated and not eradicated. We have a God who values diversity, and we are called to do the same. In addition, we have a God who, in the words of Jesus (Matt 6:25–30), cares for the smallest detail. If that is true of our God, why can't it be true of the members of Christ's body?

Reflection Questions

1. *What toxins do you believe are the greatest threat to the universal body of Christ? Which toxins have most affected your own congregation? Which toxins have most affected you?*

2. *What are some practical ways that congregations and individuals can withstand societal toxins?*

3. *What pathogens do you believe are the greatest threats to the universal body of Christ? Which pathogens have most affected your own congregation? Which pathogens have most affected you?*

4. *What are some practical ways that congregations and individuals can withstand societal pathogens?*

Chapter 8

The Body of Christ and Malignancies

AT THE ONSET OF the twenty-first century, cancer is one of the most feared conditions that a human body can develop. It is also one of the three leading causes of death in many countries.

Unlike a germ or a toxin that comes from outside the body (although the beginning of a cancer can be influenced by a toxin or a germ), it is the cells of the body that, in essence, forget that they belong to the rest of the body. Somehow, they have changed, and they multiply to create more of themselves. Left to its own devices, the single malignant cell divides to become another, and then that cell becomes another. Soon, the cell has become something the size of a golf ball, and seeds of that tumor travel to distant parts of the body, impacting organs far away from the original site. If vital organs become involved, the very life of the body is threatened.

In the human body, a cancer cell is one that does its own thing, regardless of what is good for the rest of the body. Only its own growth and progress matter. That is why it multiplies in such a way that it fails to respect any boundaries, impinging on other, still healthy, organs. A group of cancer cells will make and secrete chemicals that cause new blood vessels to grow just so they can be nourished and, presumably, grow more efficiently. In its blind quest for increasing itself at the expense of others, a cancer runs the risk of taking the life of the body that has supported it. In so

93

many ways, a cancer cell is the most selfish cell in all the human body.

Selfish though it may be, it is also a wounded cell. Cells *become* cancerous. And whether it is a genetic defect that makes the cell susceptible to toxins or pathogens, or whether it is a overwhelming burden of toxins or pathogens that no cell could overcome (e.g., a nuclear blast), a cancer cell is a very sick cell, but one that takes others with it.

Cancers are more likely in certain organs of the body, and they have predictable effects once they get started. Most cancers are preventable, and most cancers are best treated early in their course. Once a cancer progresses, there is a very real possibility of its being not treatable. To decrease the incidence of cancer, prevention is the key, with early detection the next best method for minimizing cancer's effects.

The most tragic aspect of cancer is that it is not an outsider, but it acts as if it is. A cancer cell belongs to the body, but, metaphorically speaking, has tragically lost its identity with that body. Perhaps even more tragically, the immune cells, those cells in the body that could have contained the cancer before it got too far along, did not recognize the cancer cells as aberrant and so did nothing to stop them or to keep the body healthy.

The body's immune system is that remarkable organ that protects the body from external threats, such as infectious conditions, and internal threats, such as malignancies. It does this in a variety of ways, from making certain chemicals, to making certain cells, to transporting cells from one part of the body to the part needing the help. Key to this process is the immune system's ability to recognize what belongs to the body and what doesn't belong. The immune system protects that which is healthy and belongs to the body and destroys or neutralizes that which is unhealthy or doesn't belong to the body. The mystery of cancer is that a person's immune system fails to recognize the decidedly unhealthy cells and, thus, fails to act to save the entire body.

Immune systems can, unfortunately, become overresponsive, attacking even the cells of its own bodies. These are called autoimmune diseases, and they are bad news for those who have them. As an aside, it is also why some people with COVID (especially early in the pandemic) died of multiple organ system failure; their immune systems were so primed to take out the COVID virus that they caused collateral damage in the process.

In the body of Christ, malignancies can also occur. This is not to say that a given person is a malignant cell and must be destroyed, for that would be an illegitimate appropriation of the metaphor. But, it does mean that certain conditions that are unhealthy to the body become established and literally "crowd out" or even infiltrate what was once healthy.

There are a number of scandals that fit the pattern of this "malignancy" metaphor, such as the sexual abuse of children and teens by those in authority in the church *and* the subsequent cover-ups that ensued. But there are other scandals that rock our churches. Initially healthy persons, members of the body of Christ, were victimized not only by the scandals, but also by the system that not only permitted the scandal in the first place and even covered it up when it was established. That is not the failure of one person or even persons; it is a sick system that promoted illness in the body.

Whether this illness is terminal or not depends on one's experience. For some people, directly affected by a scandal, they (and their families) left the church because they couldn't trust any longer. Just like a person who has had cancer can't quite totally trust the body that let cancer emerge in the first place, such persons can't quite trust the church system or certain leaders who defend the system.

Other people were indirectly affected by a scandal. They, themselves, were not involved, but they hear the news of one allegation after another, and they begin to wonder whether their current local church leader is upright. Some doubts might begin to creep in about beliefs that they had never questioned previously. This is akin to a cancer encroaching on otherwise healthy organs.

And then, there are the truly innocent church leaders, those who are completely appalled by scandals. They wonder if people in the pews trust them and are deeply embarrassed by the actions of those who share their vocation. They are like the healthy cells of an organ that has developed a cancer. Even though a person has lung cancer, for example, that doesn't mean that every lung cell is malignant or functioning poorly. Yet, the person with lung cancer does not fully trust those other lung cells, because he can't be sure if they are really healthy or just seem to be.

If a local church experiences a serious scandal, regardless of its nature, the membership as a whole will be affected, even if members don't know all the facts. The malignant spirit makes its move. The unity of the church community will be broken, as it becomes apparent that everyone is not working toward the same goal. Some congregations have died because of such a malignancy, and others have never been the same after the condition came to light. This can be the case in the human body as well, for if cancer doesn't kill the person, it might change her life forever and not necessarily for the better.

In such circumstances, similar to an overactive immune system, some church members are always on the lookout for any hint of trouble, effectively injuring innocent bystanders as well as those they deem to be guilty and worthy of removal. In the end, the local church body is wounded, sometimes beyond any hope of repair.

What can help in such a tragic situation? As with bodily conditions, prevention is the best way to ensure that the body stays healthy, but lacking that, early detection and treatment represents the best hope for health. And that is where the immune system comes in. The immune system is not just cells and various chemicals, but an organized system that promotes health. This system of health promotion looks for problem areas and corrects them in the ways that make the most sense. So too in the body of Christ. That means, in the example of sexual abuse, that the situation is taken seriously and the person who has been victimized (whether that be the accuser or the accused) is given all the support that she or he needs in order to get better. No amount of energy, time, or money is spared in this quest for wholeness and health. Furthermore, a system of health promotion means that anything that doesn't promote the health of a given congregation, denomination, or other church body is dealt with fairly but firmly. This is true, obviously, for sexual issues but also for other issues that hurt a congregation such as embezzlement, addictions, etc. Although the health of an individual is important, the health of the whole is also important, and steps must be taken to promote that group health . . . without overreacting or being on "high-alert" at all times.

Any human sin can represent a malignancy in the body of Christ, if it is serious and if its scope is wide enough. Rather than being mere spectators when the body of Christ is being eaten away, it would behoove us to function as parts of an immune system that want the health of the body and will actively seek the means to procure that health. We ourselves might be called to be a listening presence for those who have been directly or indirectly hurt by church leaders or church practices. We ourselves might be called to report a situation that seems to be brewing before it is a full-blown catastrophe. We ourselves might be the ones who are church leaders who must call other leaders to task. None of these tasks are easy, but all might be necessary for true healing and health to occur.

As we look at those who are accused and the accusers, it is important to recognize that both are members of the body of Christ. They both belong to us, and we belong to them. That is why factionalism is so pointless; it sets up an "us vs. them" mentality that does not serve the larger body of Christ. We all need the humility to acknowledge that every person is a sinner, although, admittedly, most of us do not commit heinous acts. Yet, some of our forebears in the faith *did* commit heinous acts. Moses killed a man. David had an adulterous affair with a married woman and then had her husband killed to cover his deed. Judas betrayed Jesus for a few coins, while Peter denied that he even knew Jesus to save his own skin. Even Paul, when he was Saul, persecuted Christians, arranging for their execution. If these figures (with the exception of Judas) represent leaders in our tradition, there is hope for us as well!

Reflection Questions

1. *Has a scandal every rocked a congregation to which you belonged? Have you ever been involved in a scandal?*

2. *What was your reaction in the church scandal? What was your reaction in a personal scandal?*

3. *Did you leave your church, or did you decide to remain? Why? Did you act as a healing presence? How so?*

4. *Did the scandal make you wary of church leaders or "politics"?*

5. *What is your "gut" reaction to the sexual abuse scandal in the church?*

6. *Have you acted as a healing presence? How so? If not, why not?*

Chapter 9

The Body of Christ and Failure of Heart

HEART DISEASE IS THE NUMBER one killer in the US. When we use the term "heart failure," we are usually referring to the condition in which the heart is incapable of pumping enough blood to meet the needs of the body. Without a healthy heart, there can be no healthy body, for it is the heart's job to ensure that oxygen-filled blood travels to all the organs, no matter how distant they are from the heart itself. Furthermore, it is the heart's job to pump waste-filled blood to the kidneys, liver, or lungs so that those organs can dispose of the waste; the heart must care for every organ, no matter how far it is located from the heart. That is the physical work of the heart.

Yet, metaphorically, the heart has emotional work of its own. We say that people have "broken hearts" when they have been deeply hurt by life. When we want someone to be courageous, we might say, "Take heart!" And, of course, we think of the heart—at least metaphorically—as the seat of love. We draw little hearts when we love someone, and on Valentine's Day, we send cards with hearts on them.

A failure of heart, then, might entail a physical condition (such as congestive heart failure, when the heart may be too bloated to pump efficiently) or an emotional one (such as one's inability to empathize or love another).

The body of Christ must have a healthy heart, for how else will it do all that it needs to do for the world? In that sense, it must reach the most distant members; sometimes, members are distant because of their own actions and sometimes because of the actions of others. It does not matter. The work of the heart of the body of Christ must pump, must infuse Christ's love to all members, regardless of where or who they are.

More importantly, however, the body must have a caring, loving heart if it is to embrace the world. In this sense, its heart must not fail. The body's heart must be modeled on the heart of Christ who loved others, even to his death.

Tragically, today, the behavior of many members of the body often makes it seem as if the entire body has a failure of heart. We are quite good when horrific events occur, rushing to the aid of those in need. Our hearts do not fail us then. In that, we have the hearts of good sprinters: able to run fast and work hard for a brief period of time.

The more insidious problem is failure of heart for the chronic, unremitting societal problems that are more like long marathons and require a marathon runner's heart. In a marathon, the runner knows that he or she cannot spend all of his or her energy at the beginning of the race, for fatigue will set in, and the race will not be successfully run. A good marathon runner knows how to pace him- or herself.

So, too, in the body of Christ. In the body, many members become fatigued when they see all the problems around. Who can blame them? In our culture, we are accustomed to quick fixes and easy solutions. If we have a pain, swallowing a pill will take care of it . . . and we should only have to take that pill once! If I ask someone to do something, that person should respond immediately. We hate waiting in lines; in fact, we hate waiting at all. We have been socialized to embrace the product while shunning the process. It's not so much that the ends justify the means; the means aren't even important.

How will we ever eradicate poverty or diseases or famine if we are looking for a quick fix? Money can't bring famines to a permanent end. How will we ever eradicate war and violence, everywhere and in all places? Money doesn't buy lasting peace. How will we ever eradicate greed and materialism? After all, these things have existed for millennia! We are not the first to experience their tenacity. Money doesn't buy happiness and certainly not joy.

So, we do what we can, but it doesn't even seem to make the slightest dent. No wonder so many of us are fatigued. No wonder so many of us are depressed, as we consider that things might not get better before they get worse . . . if they ever get better at all. It makes us want to give up before we expend too much energy. Since we can't fix things on our timetable, we retreat into our own houses, clubs, and other spheres of influence. When we are fatigued, we get consumed about our own needs; it is a matter of basic survival. After all, basic human needs include food, shelter, and rest. When we are fatigued, we haven't gotten enough rest. How could we rest—there are so many problems in the world! Let the world fix itself.

When we are consumed with our own needs, it is easy to ignore or discount others. "It's a dog eat dog world" we might say. "Every man for himself" we might think. Or, we might brag, "I pulled myself up by my bootstraps . . . let others do the same." We might begin to resonate with the ads that encourage us all to "look out for number one," especially when we realize that number one is us.

When many of us are physically fatigued, we get cranky and irritable; we are not necessarily nice people to be around. We begin to resent the demands that others place upon us. We just want to get away and get some rest. Failure to do so will lead to burnout. In burnout, we become cynical about everything, including that which once was of most importance to us.

The body of Christ does not need burned out members. Christ himself did not burn out, even though he ministered to many people with varying needs. And, after he ministered to these people, there were always more people with more needs. Yet, he did not become cynical . . . even when his closest associates failed him, those whom he healed were ungrateful or turned against him, and those whom he tried to teach insisted on his death.

When there is fatigue in the body of Christ, members might not care about other members, especially if they differ from them in some obvious way. But, this is as foolish as tired legs not caring whether or not the heart continues to beat, for if the heart stops, the legs will hurt no longer. Nor will they ever move again. This is as foolish as muscles pulsating with pain failing to care whether or not the kidneys work, for if the kidneys fail to work, toxins will build up in the body, and, in the end, damage not only the muscles but also the entire body.

So, when we do not care about other members in the body of Christ (whether they are foreigners, immigrants, or those of different racial or ethnic groups), we end up hurting ourselves, for those members are not only part of the whole but also part of us. We are part of them, and in rejecting them (or failing to care about them), we reject ourselves or fail to care about ourselves. Although conserving our energy for concerns that only affect ourselves might seem necessary, in the so-called wisdom of the world, such a stance turns out to be foolishness if it hurts us in the long run.

One person can make a difference for good or for ill. For example, a student at Virginia Tech killed thirty-two students and faculty members. A chronic lack of care and concern by others toward the gunman led, indirectly, to the death of others which, in turn, impacted an entire college campus. That one student impacted a group of over twenty-five thousand persons in community. The same is true for the body of Christ. One person can make a difference—for good or for ill. The heart of the body of Christ depends on the hearts of each of its members. We all are called to not lose heart, to not have heart failure, to love with all our heart. Success is nice, but it is not necessary. As Mother Teresa (herself one person who made a difference) is reported to have once said, "We are not called to be successful but faithful."

A healthy heart in the human body can only remain that way if it receives the proper nutrition and the right amount of exercise.

So, too, in the body of Christ. The idea of malnutrition in the body of Christ will be discussed in the next chapter. As for exercise, how have we exercised our hearts in the body of Christ?

Reflective Questions

1. *In what condition is your heart, physically and spiritually?*

2. *What are you doing to ensure the optimal health of your heart?*

3. *How do you exercise your heart to grow in love for others, both those well-known to you and those who are strangers?*

4. *Does your heart fail you when you think of certain members of the body and their behaviors? Who are they?*

5. *Does your congregation have a heart that fails or a heart that loves?*

6. *Is your congregation more likely to take heart or to lose heart?*

Chapter 10

The Body of Christ and Malnutrition

EARLIER IN THIS BOOK, the point was made that we are what we consume. If we eat foods full of sugar and fat, we risk not having the proper nutrients for our body to build cells, organs, and body systems. All body processes such as circulation and digestion depend on these proper nutrients, the lack of which can result in unhealthy bodies, ready to break down or become ill at any point, even to the point of death. If we consume healthy foods, our bodies have the proper nutrients to build healthy, well-functioning cells, organs, and tissues.

The body of Christ is nourished in several ways. Members must be persons who embrace Scripture. God's Word nourishes us by reminding us of the great things that God has done in salvation history. Indeed, the early church fathers emphasized the importance of Scripture to one's spiritual health. They encouraged believers to listen carefully to Scripture passages and let those passages soak in, like a steady rainfall. Are we convinced that Scripture is important to our spiritual health today? Other than hearing Scripture read on Sundays, how often do we read Scripture on our own? Many individuals would rather read someone's words about Scripture rather than the Scripture passages themselves, missing the direct beauty and power of the words that have the capacity to transform. After all, one person's interpretation of a passage might not touch another as deeply as the words themselves.

Furthermore, many individuals would rather read "Christian lite" or even New Age material rather than read a venerated Christian writer, because the latter is often "harder:" harder to understand and harder to live. But to give in to such temptations is akin to permitting young children to eat only foods they like rather than foods they require. If broccoli is too hard to chew, then there's always pudding! Even in Christian writing, there is always fluff, words that make absolutely no demands on the reader. Like food that melts in the mouth (instead of having to be chewed), it requires no effort and also might not provide many nutrients for one's spiritual health. Recall that Christ's words make many demands on the reader or listener.

The body of Christ is nourished by prayer. Christ was a person of prayer, and members must be persons of prayer so that they can remain connected to Christ and, through him, to his Abba. It doesn't necessarily matter what kind of prayer, as long as it is a prayer that touches the one doing the praying. Prayer is to be individual *and* communal; it is not an either-or. Each of us is called to personally grow closer to God in the way that seems best for us. Because God created us, God fully understands us and which ways of praying speak to us most clearly. That means we are to explore various forms of prayer and engage in those forms that draw us closer to God.

Yes, we also must be persons of communal prayer. Nothing reminds us of the intimate interconnectedness of the members of the body of Christ as does communal worship, especially the Eucharist. We are gathered together as a whole people, united in Christ, raising our voices in unison, praying in words and in song. Furthermore, when our communal prayer is at Eucharist, we share in the common meal, that intimate union of Christ with us and us with him, through his body and blood.

For it is the Eucharist that provides the greatest nutrition for the body of Christ. Through the Lord's own body and blood, we are not only fed for our life's journey, but we are united intimately with him. How can we maintain a close relationship with the Lord if we do not partake of the meal that he has specially prepared for us? Many of us do not always receive communion because of various reasons. Often, we feel as if we are not worthy. Well, of course we are unworthy! It is Christ who makes us worthy. In some way, it must break Christ's heart to see that his great gift is returned to him, unused and unappreciated.

Others do not receive Eucharist frequently because they think that to do so will "cheapen" it. In other words, it's only for special occasions. The comparison to the human body is apt here. Do we only eat on special occasions, like Christmas and Easter? Don't we need to eat every day? Does the fact that we eat every day make us think less of eating? Hardly! Eating can give us an appreciation of the goodness of God's creation in the wonderful foods we have available to us. Why, then, do we think that receiving Eucharist infrequently will somehow make us *more* appreciative of what Christ has done for us? Isn't this just another excuse?

Christ gave us himself as food for the journey, and we are called to partake in his body and blood. In instituting the Eucharist, Christ did not put limits on the frequency of its reception. Nor did he warn the disciples to be "worthy" when they received it. After all, the twelve disciples were present at the Eucharist's institution, including Judas, the one who would betray him; Peter, the one who would deny him; and the others who would all flee at his arrest. Hardly a worthy crew! Yet, Christ extended an invitation to his meal to all twelve, knowing how each of them would react in the next few hours of his life. If disciple unworthiness did not stand in the way of Christ offering the gift of his body and blood, how can *we* second-guess him? Of course we are not worthy, and Christ fully knows that. He loves us anyway and wants to share himself with us, precisely so that we will grow in holiness.

When we are at Eucharist, we see fellow members of the body of Christ and begin to realize that we and they share the same dreams, regrets, hopes, faults, questions, concerns, and sorrows, because they are part of the human condition, a condition with which Christ was intimately acquainted. By joining ourselves to him in Eucharist—and thereby to each other—Christ sanctifies that human condition. We become more like him. Being fed by him, we are no longer hungry, and we are better equipped to feed others. In a way, it is a bit like the story of the feeding of the five thousand in the Gospels. Christ took the initiative with a few loaves and fish. After he began the process of feeding, others were able to share what they had, so much so that there were leftovers! God's generosity is never outdone, and Christ demonstrated that clearly. As members of his body, we cannot outdo Christ in that generosity of spirit.

Once we are fed, we have the energy and strength to feed others, no matter where they are or who they are. They are beloveds of Christ, and that is all that matters. Strengthened by an intimate relationship to Christ through prayer, a close acquaintance with Scripture, and the divine meal, we are ready to act as Christ in the world, for we are one with him.

When we are well-nourished, we can move beyond ourselves, a task that is nearly impossible when we are famished, for when we are famished, we think only of our own situation, needs, and relief. Others do not matter when we are physically starving; only food matters, and only we matter. That is as true for the body of Christ as it is for the human body. For that reason, we must strive to be well-nourished. The activity of the body of Christ in the world depends on it.

Reflection Questions

1. *How are you fed in the body of Christ?*

2. *What prayer forms are most meaningful to you? How often do you engage in them?*

3. *How often do you read Scripture? If you do not do so, why not?*

4. *What are your favorite sacred readings? Have you read any classics of Christian spirituality? Why or why not?*

5. *How often do you attend mass? What do you think is the importance of communal prayer?*

6. *How often do you receive Eucharist? How important is that to your spiritual life?*

108

Chapter 11

The Body of Christ vis-à-vis the World

In the midst of World War II, Lutheran pastor Dietrich Bonhoeffer noted:

> Let the Christian remain in the world, not because of the good gifts of creation, nor because of his responsibility for the course of the world, but for the sake of the Body of the incarnate Christ and for the sake of the Church. Let him remain in the world to engage in frontal assault on it, and let him live the life of his secular calling in order to show himself as a stranger in this world all the more. But that is only possible if we are visible members of the Church . . . . The value of the secular calling for the Christian is that it provides an opportunity of living the Christian life with the support of God's grace, and of engaging more vigorously in the assault on the world and everything that it stands for . . . . The limits and claims of the secular calling are fixed by our membership in the visible Church [Body] of Christ . . . .[1]

Like the early church fathers before him, Bonhoeffer believed that where one member of the body of Christ is, there is the entire

---

1. Bonhoeffer, *Cost of Discipleship*, 297–98.

body. "It is the unity of the whole Church which makes each member what he is and the fellowship what it is . . . ."[2]

The body of Christ is meant to be *the* most positive force in the world. That requires that we take seriously the challenge to be so. It also requires that we permit ourselves to be led by the Spirit, the same Spirit which Christ promised would always be with us. The Spirit is the animating force, the inspiration, of the body of Christ.

The popular culture of many Christian nations would deny the importance of Corpus Christi spirituality. For so many of us, what is important is "I"—I personally or that which is mine, such as my family, my church, my country. "We" is only important when we are threatened by an outside force. What satisfies *me* is what I should strive for and not what satisfies others, especially if they are not known to me. Despite its protests to the contrary, the culture is materialistic and hedonistic. Furthermore, the culture creates a mind-set that believes that some hierarchies are good, and, unfortunately, that includes hierarchies of people and nations. We rarely acknowledge what the poor people of the world do for us, as we underscore what we, the wealthier countries, do for them. Sometimes, nations see it as a failure if other countries must help them, because they should be able to be self-sufficient. It is hard not to conclude that many so-called Christian nations are only nominally so.

Non-Christian nations may see many so-called Christian nations as failing to live up to their own belief system, as espoused by Christ. Do non-Christian nations see Christian nations acting as if all countries and peoples are necessary, even when poor countries cannot offer wealthier countries anything in return? Do non-Christian countries perceive a sense of superiority in many Christian countries vis-à-vis poor countries in Africa or Central America, or even wealthier, non-Christian countries? Do non-Christian countries witness greater honor (or *any* honor) given to poorer countries by Christian nations? Do they experience mutuality in solving the world's problems with the Christian countries

2. Bonhoeffer, *Cost of Discipleship*, 272.

or, instead, dominance by them? Do non-Christian nations see themselves in union with Christians nations or at odds with them, and if so, why? Although one might (probably rightly) counter that non-Christian nations probably do no better than Christian nations, those nations are not bound by the teachings of Christ as are Christian nations.

In the third part of this book, we have discussed Corpus Christi spirituality within each person and between persons. The natural next step is to take this spirituality into the world to make it something by which entire communities live. It is only then that true peace can come. Let us examine each of the attributes separately for a worldwide spirituality.

UNITY IN DIVERSITY

The world is composed of a myriad of peoples; diversity is ubiquitous. How Christian countries view diversity says much about their own fidelity to Christ. Do we see nations and peoples whose views on religion, politics, and culture differ radically from ours as enemies or fellow children of God? In this age of xenophobia, the seemingly "natural" responses are suspicion and hostility toward those whose views differ greatly from our own, seeing them as enemies who would try to do us harm. To be sure, there *are* individuals who would try to do harm to others; this is a world wounded by sin. But clearly, the world's many peoples would prefer to live in peace rather than in fear. Creating a global mind-set that we're all in this together is a first step in cultivating unity.

But practically speaking, how is that done? On a national level, world leaders speak to each other *directly* rather than speak through intermediaries—human or electronic/printed. They look for what unites them instead of searching for that which divides them, and they encourage their people to do the same, especially through cultural exchanges. They visit each other in order to give a very strong message of unity. By their words and actions, they give testimony to the belief that we are all in this together. What affects one nation likely affects others; what affects the world at large likely affects all nations to some degree.

NECESSITY OF ALL

Although it might seem far-fetched, all people are necessary in order for the world to be what it is. *All* people. The world would simply not be the world we know unless we were all present. How do we live this out? World leaders look for ways to educate their people about the necessity of those in other countries, even those in the poorest of countries, who often produce what those in the richer countries purchase. This starts in the schools, but it continues throughout life. Leaders of wealthier countries can thank those of poorer countries for the services and goods they provide to their citizens, while leaders of poorer countries can gratefully acknowledge any aid provided to them by wealthy countries. Gratitude is not servitude but grace.

INTERDEPENDENCE OF ALL

Accurate information can be provided to the citizenry of all countries about the percentage of foreign-made or foreign-grown goods available in their countries. More importantly, the amount of money that workers in poorer countries make to provide those in wealthier countries with these goods can be revealed. This is true whether the poorer country is Christian or non-Christian. Although this information might be unsettling to those in wealthier countries, it will give them a real sense of the necessity of others, whose labor permits those in the wealthier countries to continue to live in the ways to which they have become accustomed.

GREATER HONOR TO THE WEAKER

Although many Christian world leaders *do* speak about the unity and necessity of all peoples, and how interdependence is to be valued, far fewer go out of their ways to give honor to weaker countries, to praise poorer peoples. We even have a classification for this: First World countries, Second World countries, and Third World countries. Rarely are the peoples of Third World countries honored except, perhaps, by the backhanded compliment that, despite their misery, they are content. Why should anyone be content with misery? Would we be?

Giving honor to weaker countries means that the leader of a powerful country is as likely to visit a poorer country (if invited) as he or she is to visit another powerful or wealthy country. The *leader* visits, not an emissary. Giving honor to poorer, weaker countries means forgiving their indebtedness when they have no means to repay the debt. "No one ever gave us anything," citizens of wealthy countries will moan in protest. Not true, for God has given everything we have! And, even if it were true, in Corpus Christi spirituality, that is not the point. Giving honor to the weaker, poorer country means that we treat them with the kind of respect that Paul described. We look for ways to honor them and then do so.

Is this utopia? In some ways, yes, because human sinfulness will likely preclude our complete success at these measures. But, given the advances in communication and travel in our modern world, we are all closer to each other than we'd like to think, even to those in far-off lands. Through e-mail or texts, we can send messages to individuals half the world away in seconds; through modern jet travel, we can reach far-flung locations across the globe in hours, not weeks or months. Indeed, this has been *the* fear—and the reality—about infections such as COVID: once the virus mutates to infect humans directly from one person to another, it does not take months for it to spread across the globe but weeks and maybe even days.

So, the interconnectedness is reality, not utopia. How we come to terms with that can mean the difference between peace among the nations and mutual annihilation by biochemical, nuclear, or biological agents. Adopting Corpus Christi spirituality makes annihilation less likely, but does not completely eliminate the risk, for there will always be some people who fail to embrace the virtues of

Corpus Christi spirituality: unity in diversity, the necessity of all, mutual interdependence, and the provision of greater honor to the weaker rather than to the stronger, wealthier, or more powerful.

In Paul's mind, if we are truly followers of Christ, we must live Corpus Christi spirituality; that is the cost of discipleship. As Bonhoeffer noted, the cost of discipleship is high. If we embrace Christian discipleship too fervently, we might lose our earthly lives. Yet, we gain much more. We can recall Paul's message to the Roman church, words that are as true today as they were then.

> If God is for us, who can be against us? . . . What will separate us from the love of Christ? Will anguish, or distress, or persecution, or famine, or nakedness, or peril, or the sword? . . . No, in all these things , we conquer overwhelmingly through him who loved us. For I am convinced that neither death, nor life, nor angels, nor principalities, nor present things, nor future things, nor powers, nor height, nor depth, nor any other creature will be able to separate us from the love of God in Christ Jesus our Lord. (Rom 8:31b, 35–39)

True followers of Christ need not fear. Faithfulness to Christ, not worldly success according to the world's standards, is the measuring rod. To quote Bonhoeffer:

> The member of the Body of Christ . . . must give the world a visible proof of his calling, not only by sharing in the Church's worship and discipline, but also through the new fellowship of brotherly living. If the world despises one of the brethren, the Christian will love and serve him. If the world does him violence, the Christian will succour and comfort him. If the world dishonours and insults him, the Christian will sacrifice his own honour to cover his . . . shame. Where the world seeks gain, the Christian will renounce it. Where the world exploits, he will dispossess himself, and where the world oppresses, he will stoop down and raise up the oppressed. If the world refuses justice, the Christian will pursue mercy, and if the world takes refuge in lies, he will open his mouth for the [mute], and bear testimony to the truth.

> For the sake of the [other] . . . .he will renounce all fellowship with the world.[3]

This means that suffering is a very real part of Corpus Christi spirituality. Joined to Christ, we cannot help but suffer when he is reviled even to this day. Bonhoeffer noted: "In the fellowship of the crucified and glorified body of Christ, we participate in his suffering and glory. His cross is the burden which is laid on his Body, the Church. All the sufferings borne beneath this cross are the sufferings of Christ himself."[4]

And there are many sufferings borne beneath the cross, sufferings initiated by human actions and sufferings initiated by forces in nature. Joined to each other, we cannot help but suffer when those intimately united with Christ and we suffer, and this suffering is unavoidable if we take our membership in the body of Christ seriously. That is the bad news. The good news is that our own suffering might—in some way—bring about God's reign in ways that we can't even imagine. Bonhoeffer said it well:

> For while it is true that only the suffering of Christ himself can atone for sin . . . yet to some, who are not ashamed of their fellowship in his body, he vouchsafes the immeasurable grace and privilege of suffering "for him" as he did for them . . . no higher privilege can the Christian enjoy, than to suffer "for Christ" . . . . Although Christ has fulfilled all the vicarious suffering necessary for our redemption, his suffering on earth is not finished yet. He has, in his grace, left a residue of suffering for his Church to fulfill in the interval before his Second Coming (Col. 1.24). This suffering is allowed to benefit the Body of Christ, the Church. Whether we have any right to assume that this suffering has power to atone for sin (cf. I Pet. 4.1), we have no means of knowing. But we do at least know that the man who suffers in the power of the body of Christ suffers in a representative capacity "for" the Church, the Body of Christ, being privileged to endure himself what others are spared . . . . The Body

3. Bonhoeffer, *Cost of Discipleship*, 289.

4. Bonhoeffer, *Cost of Discipleship*, 272.

of Christ has its own allotted portion of suffering. God grants one man the grace to bear special suffering in place of another, and this suffering must at all costs be endured and overcome . . . . Such vicarious activity and passivity on the part of the members of the Body is the very life of Christ, who wills to be formed in his members. (Gal 4.19)[5]

In closing, there are no better words than those of St. Teresa of Avila, words quoted by Webb-Mitchell.[6]

Christ has no body now but yours,
No hands but yours,
No feet but yours.
Yours are the eyes through which
Christ's compassion must look out to the world.
Yours are the feet with which
He is to go about doing good.
Yours are the hands with which
He is to bless us now.

Reflection Questions

1. *Which peoples in your city, country, or the world seem outside the reach of the body of Christ?*

2. *What should those in wealthier countries do (practically speaking) in order to remember that the body of Christ includes people from all countries, even the poorest or those countries considered to be enemies?*

3. *What should those in poorer countries do (practically speaking) in order to remember that the body of Christ includes people from all countries, even the wealthiest or those countries considered to be enemies?*

4. *What can YOU do—here and now—to start that process?*

5. Bonhoeffer, *Cost of Discipleship*, 273–74.
6. Webb-Mitchell, *Christly Gestures*, 126.

APPENDIX

Selected Early Church Fathers' Reflections on the Body of Christ
Christ's Relationship to His Members

ALTHOUGH THE ACTUAL TERM "body of Christ" was not always used by early fathers of the church, their writings consistently spoke of the unity of all persons in Christ. The earliest writings are more about Christ than the members and underscore Christ's union with the members of his body more so than the unity of members with each other. This is true of many of the documents whose authors are unknown from the first hundred years or so of the Christian era, such as the Pastor of Hermas, Second Epistle of Clement, and the Epistle of Barnabas.

Many of the writings up to the year 300 CE were written under two circumstances: persecution of the Christians by the Roman government and/or emergence of heretical movements. The early fathers of the church were in a siege mentality, whether besieged from without or from within. Hence, there is much emphasis on church structure, hierarchy, legitimate authority, and fundamental beliefs; adherence to these aspects of the church brings one into unity with other Christians.

Quotations are taken from Emile Mersch's book *The Whole Christ.*

BISHOP CLEMENT OF ROME:

Around 100 CE, Clement of Rome wrote that those who had divergent views and who had broken away from the church (i.e., the schismatics of the day) were tearing the body of Christ apart when they "disrupted" the unity of the church.[1]

BISHOP IGNATIUS OF ANTIOCH:

In the midst of persecutions by imperial Rome, Ignatius of Antioch (35-107 CE) emphasized the unity of Christ, with each member of the body joined to him, the head.[2] For Ignatius, visible church unity was situated in the persons of the bishop and clergy,[3] who extended it to those whom they served; visible unity was an outward sign of "spiritual" unity between Christ and his church.[4]

BISHOP IRENAEUS OF LYONS:

During the time of his episcopacy, Irenaeus of Lyons (130–202 CE) saw many waves of persecution and various heresies. He believed that those who disagreed with church teachings, "lacerate and divide the great and glorious body of Christ, and do all in their power to kill it . . . The true gnosis [i.e., knowledge] is the doctrine of the apostles, and the ancient organization of the church throughout the world, and the character of the body of Christ according to the succession of the bishops to whom the apostles entrusted each of the local churches."[5] Thus, the theme of unity through *persons* (i.e.,

1. Mersch, *Whole Christ,* 214.
2. Mersch, *Whole Christ,* 217.
3. Mersch, *Whole Christ,* 218.
4. Mersch, *Whole Christ,* 219.
5. Mersch, *Whole Christ,* 235–36.

apostles to bishops to believers) became paramount, especially in combating heretical movements that denied the importance of certain offices. Furthermore, since the unity of persons conveyed their unity of beliefs, it was also used in opposing heretical movements that denied certain beliefs about Christ himself.

One of these was Christ's relationship to the faithful. Irenaeus believed that there is an "interchange" between Christ and the members of his body. Mersch reflects on this thought:

> We receive in ourselves the outpouring of the glories of Christ, while He takes our infirmities into Himself, in order to destroy them . . . So truly do we possess all things in common with Him, that from what we are it is possible to infer what He had to be, just as it is possible to see, from what He is, what we in turn are destined one day to be.[6]

ORIGEN OF THE ALEXANDRIAN SCHOOL:

Origen (185–254 CE), a major force in the School of Alexandria and attracted to mysticism, spoke of the intimate relationship of believers and Christ, especially with regard to the resurrection of those united to him.

> As the visible body of Jesus was nailed to the cross and buried, and then raised up, so the whole body of Christ's saints is nailed with Him to the cross and now no longer lives . . . But when the resurrection of this true and complete body takes place, then the members of Christ, which now resemble dry bones, shall be united bone to bone and joint to joint, each will have its proper place . . . Thus shall the many members be one body, since all the members will belong to the same body.[7]

Origen believed that Christ was mystically united with all people and will receive his glory when we do. He was soundly criticized for this, but he explained it in terms of Christ's love:

6. Mersch, *Whole Christ*, 241.

7. Mersch, *Whole Christ*, 256.

> Since we are all His body, and are called His members,
> therefore as long as some of us are not yet perfectly sub-
> ject [to God], He Himself is said not to be subject. . . . He
> does not wish to receive His perfect glory without thee,
> that is, without His people who are His body and His
> members.[8]

For Origen, the body of Christ was in a state of development
and would never reach perfection in this life.

> . . . we are as yet His members and His bones only in an
> imperfect manner . . . [having] not the jointure of charity,
> nor the sinews of patience, nor the veins of a living spirit,
> not the vigor of faith. But when He came who was sent
> to gather what was dispersed and to bind together what
> was scattered, joining bone to bone and joint to joint, He
> began to build the holy body of the Church.[9]

BISHOP CYPRIAN OF CARTHAGE:

In the midst of persecutions and the temptation to deny one's faith
to save one's life, Cyprian of Carthage (?–258 CE) pleaded for unity.

> For when the Lord tells us that this bread, formed by
> the union of many grains, is His Body, He signifies that
> the whole Christian people which He bears in Himself,
> is one. And when He says that the wine, pressed from
> many grapes to form a single liquid, is His Blood, He
> again signifies that our flock is one through the union
> of many together. . . . So perfectly are the water and wine
> united in the cup of the Lord that they cannot be sepa-
> rated. In like manner, the Church, that is the multitude
> of the faithful united in the Church and persevering in
> faith, can never be separated from Christ . . . And as the
> cup of the Lord is neither water alone nor wine alone but
> a mixture of the two, so too neither flour alone nor water
> alone can become the Body of Christ. The two must be
> mixed together, they must adhere in one form loaf. Thus
> we see that the sacrament itself symbolizes the unity of

8. Mersch, *Whole Christ*, 259.

9. Mersch, *Whole Christ*, 260.

the Christian people. As many grains are gathered and ground and kneaded together to form one bread, let us realize that we too are one body in Christ, the heavenly Bread, to whom we are joined and united.[10]

BISHOP ATHANASIUS OF ALEXANDRIA:

By the time of Athanasius of Alexandria (328–373 CE), Christianity was no longer subject to persecution by the Romans; the immediate external threat had been removed, but there were still heretical movements, internal threats. Accordingly, he highlighted the body of Christ in many of his writings against heretics and pagans. In "Against the Pagans," he wrote,

> The Greek philosophers say that the world is a great body. And in this, they are right. For we see that the world and its parts are sensible things. If, then, the word of God resides in this world, which is a body; if He is present in each and every thing, is there anything strange or absurd in our claim that the Word is present in man?[11]

At the time, there was debate as to whether Christ was both fully human and fully divine. Because the orthodox belief was (and still is) that he is both, if He is truly united with believers, Mersch summarizes Athanasius: "Christ is so truly one with us that He can communicate His divinity to us . . ."[12] So intimate is that union that Athanasius could say "Christ bore our body" and we "are in His body."[13]

BISHOP HILARY OF POITIERS:

Like Athanasius, Hilary of Poitiers (315–368 CE) believed that there was a continuity between Christ and the members of his

10. Mersch, *Whole Christ*, 378–79.
11. Mersch, *Whole Christ*, 264.
12. Mersch, *Whole Christ*, 272.
13. Mersch, *Whole Christ*, 280.

body; people were actually incorporated into Christ and Christ incorporated into them, and this is precisely what imparted divinity to human beings. He said, "Our Lord is transfused into the bodies of each of the faithful . . . all humanity is contained in Him . . . He is like a city, and by our union with His Flesh we are his inhabitants."[14] Mersch concludes: "It is the ancient teaching of Scripture and Tradition that Christ abides in us and we in Him." [15]

Naturally, Christ is united with his people through the gift of himself in the Eucharist. But, he was first united with his people through the incarnation. In the act of becoming human, Christ knew, firsthand, the joys and sufferings of humanity. He truly knew what it was to be tired, hungry, and thirsty. Furthermore, his knowledge and experience of suffering did not end at his death, if he truly is one with his members.

BISHOP GREGORY NAZIANZEN OF CAPPADOCIA:

Gregory Nazianzen of Cappadocia (325–389 CE) noted that Christ still suffers today:

> . . . He willed to sleep, in order to bless our sleep; He willed to be weary, in order to bless our weariness; He willed to weep, in order to give merit to our tears . . . . His generously extended hands against those that reach out with greed; His nail-pierced hands against those that are fallen in discouragement.[16]

Furthermore, Gregory wrote these famous words that have resonated throughout the centuries: "Let us become like Christ, since Christ also became like us. Let us become gods for Him, since He became a man for us"[17] *"For what is not assumed [by Christ] is*

14. Mersch, *Whole Christ*, 293.

15. Mersch, *Whole Christ*, 295.

16. Mersch, *Whole Christ*, 311.

17. Mersch, *Whole Christ*, 312.

not saved; that alone is saved which is united with God."[18] In other words, if Christ was not fully human and did not experience what we experience, human beings (and their condition) are not really saved.

BISHOP GREGORY OF NYSSA:

A fellow Cappadocian, Gregory of Nyssa (?–386 CE) expanded this belief of Christ's intimate union with believers to include *all* creation.

> Since He is in all, He takes into Himself all who are united with Him by the participation of His body; He makes them all members of His body, in such wise that the many members are but one body . . . Thus all creation becomes one body, all are grafted one upon the other . . . His body, as we have often said, is the whole of humankind, to which he has united himself.[19]

> In our body, whatever is experienced by one of the senses is felt in the whole organism. Similarly, as if all human nature were a single living being, the resurrection of one of its members extends through the entire body, and because of the continuity and unity of our nature, it passes from a part to the whole body.[20]

PATRIARCH CYRIL OF ALEXANDRIA:

Cyril of Alexandria (375–444 CE) emphasized the incarnation, that the Word became flesh. The purpose of this incarnation was the ultimate divinization of humankind. Because we are in Christ, we receive life and our spirit through this intimate contact with him. Cyril wrote,

18. Mersch, *Whole Christ*, 313.

19. Mersch, *Whole Christ*, 319.

20. Mersch, *Whole Christ*, 321.

> If honey can communicate its perfection to foods that are not naturally sweet, and if it can transform into its own nature whatsoever is mingled with it, it is not absurd to say that the life-giving nature of the Word could not raise to His own perfection the body in which He dwells.[21]

> Through one body, which is His own, He blesses, by a mysterious communion, those who believe in Him, and He makes them concoporeal with Himself and with one another . . . we become one body, since there can be no division in Christ. For this reason is the Church called the body of Christ, and we severally His members . . .[22]

In other words, though members of the one body, no one loses his or her individuality by that membership.

BISHOP AUGUSTINE OF HIPPO:

Response to various heretics

Against the heretical Donatists (those who denounced clergy who had renounced their faith during the persecutions and denied the validity of their sacraments), Augustine wrote, "What has the Church done to thee that thou shouldst wish to decapitate her? Thou wouldst take away her Head, and believe in the Head alone, despising the body. Vain is thy service, and false thy devotion to the Head. For to sever it from the body is an injury to both Head and body."[23]

Again, against the Donatists who held that Christ (who instituted the sacraments) was to be revered but those sacraments depended on the worthiness of human persons, Augustine believed that they separated Christ not only from the sacraments but also from his body, the church, denying Christ's unity with his church. Eager to have the unity that Christ so desired ("That all may be one," John 17:21), Augustine pleaded with those who separated

21. Mersch, *Whole Christ*, 340.
22. Mersch, *Whole Christ*, 346.
23. Mersch, *Whole Christ*, 420.

themselves from the church: "Come brothers, please, and be engrafted on the vine; we grieve to see you lying there, cut off what is thine."[24]

Against the heretical Pelagians (who denied that Christ's death was not redemptive, since humankind was essentially good and not in need of redemption), Augustine wrote: "Let us therefore understand that our Head is the very source of grace; from Him grace flows into all His members, according to the capacity of each."[25] We are not sinless; nor are we the source of grace for ourselves. That belongs to Christ, the head.

Perspective on the Unity of Christ and Members

From the aforementioned quotes, it is obvious that Augustine believed that unity of Christ and members was real and profound. He repeated the theme in multiple ways, and the following are a few examples.

> All men are one man in Christ, and the unity of the Christians constitutes but one man . . . And this man is all men, and all men are this man; for all are one, since Christ is one.[26]

In his sermon on Psalm 90, Augustine said,

> Our Lord Jesus Christ . . . is Head and body . . . His body is the Church, not simply the Church that is in this particular place, but both the Church that is here and the Church which extends over the whole earth; not simply the Church that is living today, but the whole race of saints, from Abel down to all those who will ever be born and will believe in Christ until the end of the world, for all belong to one city. This city is the body of Christ . . . This is the whole Christ: Christ united with the

24. Mersch, *Whole Christ*, 395.

25. Mersch, *Whole Christ*, 405.

26. Mersch, *Whole Christ*, 414.

> Church. . . . Not only are we become Christians, but we are become Christ . . . we are made Christ![27]

> Since the whole Christ is Head and body, let us so listen to the voice of the Head that we may also hear the body speak . . . .[28]

Augustine imagines Christ saying,

> "I sanctify them in Myself as Myself, since in Me they too are Myself." . . . we are He, since we are His body and since He was made man in order to be our Head.[29]

> If we consider ourselves, if we think of His body, we shall see that He is ourselves. For if we were not He, it would not be true that "inasmuch as ye did it to one of these My brethren, ye did it to me" (Mt 25:40). If we were not He, these words would not be true: "Saul, Saul, why dost thou persecute Me?" (Acts 9:4). Therefore, we too are He, because we are His members, because we are His body, because He is our Head, because the whole Christ is Head and body. . . . We are members of this Head, and the body cannot be decapitated. If the Head is in glory forever, so too are the members in glory forever.[30]

Strengthening of the Body by the Eucharist

As a good pastor, Augustine emphasized the importance of Eucharist as the sacrament of unity in the church, of the body of Christ. This union with Christ imparts holiness to his sinful members by drawing us ever closer to the source of our holiness.

> For you hear the words: "The body of Christ," and you answer "Amen." Be therefore members of Christ, that your "Amen" may be true . . . What is this one bread? It is one body formed of many. Remember that bread is not

27. Mersch, *Whole Christ*, 415.

28. Mersch, *Whole Christ*, 421.

29. Mersch, *Whole Christ*, 432.

30. Mersch, *Whole Christ*, 433.

made of one grain but of many . . . Be what you see, and receive what you are . . . Many grapes hang from the vine, but the juice of all the grapes is fused into unity.[31]

Perspective on the Trinity's Love for the Body

In the incarnation of Christ, the divine and human became intimately joined. God so loved us that Christ became one of us. Because the Father loves Christ, the Father loves all who are one with Christ, because Christ cannot be divided. The Father cannot love only a part of Christ but not another part. About that love, Augustine wrote:

> God, who loves His Son, cannot do otherwise than love the members of His Son. Nor has He any other reason for loving them except that He loves the Son . . . Us He loves because we are members of His well-beloved Son. And, that we might become members, He loved us before we came into existence . . . And since God hates none of the things He has made, who can adequately describe how dearly He loves the members of His Only-begotten Son? Thus, the love wherewith the Father loves the Son is also in us . . . because we are members of the Son; we are loved in Him, because the Son is loved wholly, Head and body.[32]

31. Mersch, *Whole Christ*, 426–27.
32. Mersch, *Whole Christ*, 435.

Bibliography

Banks, Robert. *Paul's Idea of Community: The Early House Churches in Their Historical Setting*. Grand Rapids: Eerdmans, 1980.

Barrett, C. K. *A Commentary on the Epistle to the Romans*. London: A & C Black, 1991.

Bartlett, David. *Romans*. Westminster Bible Commentary. Louisville: Westminster John Knox, 1995.

Blue Letter Bible. "O Israel" (word search). https://www.blueletterbible.org/search/search.cfm?Criteria=%22O+Israel%22&t=KJV#s=s_primary_0_1.

Bonhoeffer, Dietrich. *The Cost of Discipleship*. New York: Macmillan, 1963.

Brookins, Timothy. *Reading 1 Corinthians: A Literary and Theological Commentary*. Reading the New Testament 2nd Series. Macon, GA: Smyth & Helwys, 2020.

Bultema, Harry. "The Soma or Body." www.bereanbiblesociety.org/the-soma-or-body.

Calvin, John. *Commentary on the Epistle to the Romans*. Translated by Francis Sibson. Philadelphia: J. Whetham, 1836.

———. *The Epistles of Paul the Apostle to the Romans and to the Thessalonians*. Calvin's Commentaries 8. Translated by Ross Mackenzie. Grand Rapids: Eerdmans, 1995.

Cerfaux, L. *The Church in the Theology of St. Paul*. Translated by Geoffrey Webb and Adrian Walker. New York: Herder & Herder, 1959.

Cole, Alan. *The Body of Christ: A New Testament Image of the Church*. Christian Foundations. Philadelphia: Westminster, 1964.

Dauphinais, Michael. "The Common Good and the Body of Christ: St. Thomas Aquinas and the Catholic Worker Movement." *Houston Catholic Worker* 17.6, November 1997. www.cjd.org/1997/11/01/the-common-good-and-the-body-of-christ-st-thomas-aquinas-and-the-catholic-worker-movement.

Fee, Gordon. *The First Epistle to the Corinthians*. Grand Rapids: Eerdmans, 1987.

Flannery, Austin, ed. *Vatican II: Volume 1 The Conciliar and Post Conciliar Documents*. Northport, NY: Costello, 1998.

BIBLIOGRAPHY

Garland, David. *1 Corinthians*. Baker Exegetical Commentary on the New Testament. Grand Rapids: Baker Academic, 2003.

Gibbs, Laura. *Aesop's Fables*. Translated by Laura Gibbs. Oxford: Oxford University Press, 2002.

Gorman, Michael. *Apostle of the Crucified Lord: A Theological Introduction to Paul and His Letters*. Grand Rapids: Eerdmans, 2004.

————. *Cruciformity: Paul's Narrative Spirituality of the Cross*. Grand Rapids: Eerdmans, 2001.

Haight, Roger. *Christian Community in History: Volume I Historical Ecclesiology*. New York: Continuum, 2004.

Hale, David. "Analogy of the Body Politic" In *Dictionary of the History of Ideas*. https://xtf.lib.virginia.edu/xtf/view?docId=DicHist/uvaBook/tei/DicHist1.xml&query=Dictionary%20of%20the%20History%20of%20Ideas.

Hays, Richard. *First Corinthians*. Interpretation, A Bible Commentary for Teaching and Preaching. Louisville: John Knox, 1997.

Hollingshead, James: *The Household of Caesar and the Body of Christ: A Political Interpretation of the Letters from Paul*. Lanham, MD: University Press of America, 1998.

Horsley, Richard. *1 Corinthians*. Abingdon New Testament Commentaries. Nashville: Abingdon, 1998.

Keck, Leander. *Romans*. Abingdon New Testament Commentaries. Nashville: Abingdon, 2005.

Kovacs, Judith. *1 Corinthians: Interpreted by Early Christian Commentators*. The Church's Bible. Translated and edited by Judith Kovacs. Grand Rapids: Eerdmans, 2005.

Lusk, Rich. "Calvin on Pastor and Community." http://hornes.org/theologia/rich-lusk/calvin-on-the-pastor-and-community.

MacDonald, Margaret. *Colossians and Ephesians*. Sacra Pagina 17. Collegeville, MN: Liturgical, 2000.

Martin, Dale. *The Corinthian Body*. New Haven: Yale University Press, 1995.

Mersch, Emile. *The Whole Christ: The Historical Development of the Doctrine of the Mystical Body of Christ in Scripture and Tradition*. Translated by John Kelly. Eugene, OR: Wipf and Stock, 2011.

Milner, Benjamin. *Calvin's Doctrine of the Church*. Studies in the History of Christian Thought 5. Leiden: EJ Brill Archive, 1970.

Moo, Douglas. *The Epistle to the Romans*. Grand Rapids: Eerdmans, 1996.

Myers, Edward. "Essay XIX The Mystical Body of Christ." www.marys-touch.com/Teaching/XIX.

Oster, RE. *1 Corinthians*. NIV Commentary. Joplin, MO: College Press, 1995.

Parsch, Pius. *We Are Christ's Body*. Translated by Clifford Howell. Notre Dame, IN: Fides, 1962.

Thiessen, Gerd. *Psychological Aspects of Pauline Theology*. Translated by John Galvin. Philadelphia: Fortress, 1987.

Thiselton, Anthony. *The First Epistle to the Corinthians: A Commentary on the Greek Text*. Grand Rapids: Eerdmans, 2000.

Webb-Mitchell, Brett: *Christly Gestures: Learning to Be Members of the Body of Christ*. Grand Rapids: Eerdmans, 2003.

Williams, David. *Paul's Metaphors: Their Context and Character*. Peabody, MA: Hendrickson, 1999.

Witherington, Ben. *Conflict and Community in Corinth: A Socio-Rhetorical Commentary on 1 and 2 Corinthians*. Grand Rapids: Eerdmans, 1995.

9 781666 765427